THIS NATION UNDER GOD

for us to be here dedicated to the great task remaining before us— that from these honored dead we take increased devotion to the cause for which they here gave the last full measure of devotion— that we here highly resolve that these dead shall not have died in vain; that this nation shall have a new birth of freedom; and that this government of the people, by the people, for the people, shall not perish from the earth.

Courtesy of the Library of Congress and furnished to the author by Dr. Wayne C. Grover, Archivist of the United States.

The above is a photostatic copy of the notes President Lincoln prepared in his own handwriting and used when he delivered his Gettysburg Address. It will be noted that the words of his which we are using as the title of this book are lacking. "Under God" Lincoln inserted extemporaneously by the inspiration of the occasion. As every American thrills with a new hearing of Lincoln's words delivered four score and seven years ago, it is easy to understand how inspiration could grip his soul and guide his tongue as he stood speaking.

THIS NATION UNDER GOD

by

ELBERT D. THOMAS

New York

HARPER & BROTHERS PUBLISHERS

TO ETHEL
November 6

Other Books by the Same Author

SUKUI NO MICHI (in Japanese)

CHINESE POLITICAL THOUGHT

WORLD UNITY THROUGH STUDY OF HISTORY

THOMAS JEFFERSON, WORLD CITIZEN

THE FOUR FEARS

ACKNOWLEDGMENTS

I thank the members of my overworked staff, who have to bear the brunt of every extra job I undertake. I thank especially Mr. Alan Robert Murray, author of *What the Constitution Says*, who worked with me in the development of my theme and shared in the writing of the finished work.

Mr. Murray, as a member of the office of the Co-ordinator of Information, co-operated in my first message to the Japanese people in December, 1941. During the whole war and for nearly a year after V-J Day, Mr. Murray and his associates in the Office of War Information helped with my messages. They should share whatever credit is given to me for my efforts in psychological warfare.

ELBERT D. THOMAS

CONTENTS

I. IS OURS A LAND OF DESTINY?

IS OURS A LAND OF DESTINY?

THE SEED from which this little book grew was planted in Philadelphia during 1944, when I was a delegate to the conference of the International Labor Organization, at which the Declaration of Philadelphia was written.

This great declaration, which speaks as mightily for all the free peoples of the world as did our own earlier declaration for our freedom, was being drafted by representatives of most of the nations of the world. To me it seemed a natural evolutionary development of what had taken place in Philadelphia more than a century and a half before.

I recalled the toasts of the people of Philadelphia at their first meeting after the approval of the Constitution. There were two, one to the United States of America and the other to freedom for all mankind.

In a fundamental sense, my feeling that this was a proper sequence of events came from my religious training. I was schooled in the Mormon faith, and our Articles of Faith and religious literature are filled with expressions marking the United States as the land of destiny, bringing to the concept of destiny the basic belief that God's purposes are being evolved in our historical development and that His purposes are not to glorify us, but to enrich the whole world. Not Mormons alone, but all Protestants, Catholics and Jews unite in this basic belief. The concept of revelation itself is a concept which accepts literally the notion of the purposefulness of creation and man's place in the divine scheme.

An old friend of mine, Bishop Francis Joseph Haas of the Roman Catholic Church, who came to Philadelphia at that time, suggested to me that in some way or other God should be mentioned in the Philadelphia Declaration, for surely what was being done in the world, if it were to last, must be in harmony with God's purposes. I naturally concurred, and promised to see what I could do about it. I thought the suggestion would be accepted almost immediately as a matter of course.

But it was not. Objections were made to every phrase I could devise, even such mild ones as "in the providence of God." Eventually I proposed what is commonly used in Chinese literature, "the direction of Heaven," but this fared no better. As a last try, I turned to a variation of an expression I had used once in describing Columbus' epoch-making voyage across the Atlantic, "Under Heaven Columbus sailed," and this too was declined. The representatives of nearly all the world's nations, while professing a belief in God, objected to any hint of such a belief in the text of the declaration.

Afterward in discussing the matter quietly, some delegates suggested that the decision was caused by the spread of a communistic spirit in the world. Others pointed out that the Constitution of the United States does not mention God, and gave credit for much of our country's success to the fact that all statements of theories about destiny and God's purposes had been omitted. They argued that our history has shown that the ideal of separation of Church

[4]

and State is best preserved when religious references are left out of fundamental laws.

The whole experience moved me to wonder if the belief in the United States as a land of destiny, specially selected by God for the accomplishment of His purposes, has played an important part in our development.

Has this belief helped us to go forward? Has it hindered us in the path or beguiled us into straying from it? Has it strengthened our ideals of democracy, liberty and equal justice, or conflicted with them? Has it been merely a pious and perfunctory gesture, or a vital force in the lives of our people and our leaders?

To provide the material for full answers to these questions would require years of historical study and the writing of many volumes. It occurred to me that by a relatively simple device, a significant guidepost at least could be discovered. The device consisted in the examination of public utterances of the thirty-two men who have been the Presidents of the United States, and the selection from those utterances of characteristic expressions about God and our destiny. The addition of relevant dates and a few facts about the Presidents and the status of the nation at the times the expressions were made, throws the quotations into interesting perspective.

Because the United States is pre-eminently a nation that has not been dominated by its political leaders, I have also written an account of our people throughout the years of our national life, in terms of their struggles and advances arising from religious and democratic impulses. This is by no means a complete history of the United States, but I

[5]

hope the reader will find in this account a novel—and perhaps exciting—approach to understanding what Lincoln meant by "this nation, under God."

Finally, I have written under the title, "Our Unique Heritage," a brief and personal interpretation of the place of the United States in the world—the past and present impact of other nations on us and our past and present impact on the world—with the purpose of our comprehending what lies ahead for the world. It is only as we think in terms of the whole world that each of us today can be a whole person.

I chose to use quotations from the Presidents, not because they have been necessarily the greatest men of their periods, but because more nearly than any other men in the entire history of the world they have represented the attitudes, desires and beliefs of a whole people over a considerable period of time. They attained the office of President by procedures set up by the people themselves, and, in almost every case, through the votes of more Americans than rival candidates received. As individuals they differed widely; some were strong, some weak; some were wise, some perhaps foolish; some what we call today liberal or even radical, others what we call conservative or even reactionary. But as Presidents they have personified a philosophy of government and a concept of democracy, religion and—to use a much-battered word—Americanism, that was shared by the bulk of the people whose servants they have been.

A surface objection to the value of a compilation of quotations about God and our destiny from the messages and addresses of our Presidents may arise from the impres-

[6]

sion that a similar compilation of statements by the heads of government of almost any country in the world would look and sound about the same as this one. Whether in ancient or in modern times, in Oriental or in Occidental lands, appropriate tributes to a Creator have nearly always been made at public functions, and a specially excellent relationship between the Creator and the particular ruler and his people has nearly always been claimed or implied. If that is the case, then this compilation proves nothing.

I call this a surface objection because I think the reader will find as he actually studies what our Presidents have said what I found in the same way, that whatever else they may be, these statements are not at all like those made in other countries. He will find, perhaps to his surprise, that ingrained in American tradition and philosophy is a unique approach to religion, and that these statements reveal this. A few of them may appear to be no more than formal acknowledgments of the goodness and power of God; but the whole body of them forms an impressive and memorable commentary and example of this unique approach.

That these quotations *prove* nothing, however, is true. My purpose in selecting them was not to persuade anybody of anything. It was merely to provide a guidepost, as I have called it, pointing to a better understanding of the place of the religious beliefs of Americans in the past, present and future of our country and the world.

This book is not intended primarily for students and scholars in the fields of theology, philosophy or government, though I hope some of them may find it a useful tool. It is intended for human beings living through difficult days in which doubts and fears play a large part. The series of questions evoked in my mind by the experience in Philadelphia are not just intellectual or technical problems.

They reach deep into the lives of all of us. Many are led to wonder if religion has any validity, if God is really all-powerful—indeed, if He really exists at all—and if chaos and destruction do not face the human race. For these and other human beings in perplexity, I think this compilation has much to offer.

Merely for background purposes I am setting down here informally some personal thoughts about three questions which I think the quotations and the other material in this book may help to answer. The questions are these:

Can a sincere and intelligent person believe in God and religion today?

What is the relationship between religion and American democratic principles?

Can belief in the theory of a "chosen people" and a God-inspired "national destiny" be squared with the ideals of universal brotherhood and equal rights for all?

Can a Sincere and Intelligent Person Believe in God and Religion Today?

As these words are written, people all over the world are engaged in the task of repairing the frightful damage done to their lands, their homes, their bodies and their souls during the past decade—the damage done by groups who proclaimed they were conducting holy crusades. In Germany, Italy and Japan not long ago, self-named

ened self-interest" nor "practical ethics" can make effective substitutes.

There must be faith without proof and hope beyond reason and love above advantage, or mankind will indeed perish.

Each of us sooner or later in life comes face to face with those overwhelming mysteries of the existence of human beings, birth and death, and with other evidence of a physical universe so far beyond our grasp that we cannot know even the hem of its skirt. These realities cannot be dismissed by giving them labels. They cannot be penetrated by our denying that there is more to them than we can fathom with our reason. That is why faith in God and His power and goodness are worth while, for this faith brings us not only peace of mind but also a closer approach to reality than anything else in the universe.

What Is the Relationship between Religion and American Democratic Principles?

A great deal of misunderstanding, it seems to me, has come from the separation of Church and State in the United States. The erroneous impression exists in some quarters that this step represented a turning away from religion, a minimizing of its importance in the day-to-day affairs of men. Actually, this step was based on an abiding belief in God and a determination to prevent men from distorting such a belief into a form of oppression. But unless we preserve the belief, we lose all the value of the unique American approach to religion.

The United States was the first nation on earth to recognize fully the dignity, rights and privileges of each individual, and to protect the individual's rights to freedom of religion. It was also the first nation to deny that any person or body of people possesses a divine right to rule over any other person or body of people. I make these statements with full awareness that religious toleration was practiced in some countries before the birth of the United States, and that some representative governments came into being before our own. But the freedom of religion accomplished in the United States was different from what was formerly understood by that term. It was not just the tolerance of those who are right for those in error.

George Washington best expressed it in his famous words to the Jewish congregation at Newport:

It is now no more that toleration is spoken of, as if it was by the indulgence of one class of the people, that another enjoyed the exercise of their inherent and natural rights. For happily the government of the United States, which gives to bigotry no sanction, to persecution no assistance, requires only that they who live under its protection should demean themselves as good citizens, in giving it on all occasions their effectual support.

Different also from anything known before was the stand on alleged God-given rights to dominate or rule people. The Constitution of the United States set forth a fundamental advance from the position taken in the Declaration of Independence, or rather, carried into practice what was only implicit in the former document.

The Declaration of Independence proclaimed that governments derive their "just powers from the consent of the governed." The Constitution proclaimed the right of the people to be their own governors, not just the governed who consent to the rule of specially selected individuals or groups. It would not be amiss to call our Constitution, for this reason, a companion declaration, the Declaration of Self-Government.

The separation of Church and State was not simply an interesting feature of our governmental structure. It was an integral part of the very fabric of our concept of a democratic state. The dignity of the individual, derived from religion, and the authority of the people, also derived from religion, cannot be maintained if any power above that of the individual or of the people as a whole is the legal arbiter or director of the actions of human beings. The supreme principle of democratic government is the sovereignty of the people.

Religion as an inspiration, religion as a guide to personal conduct, religion as the source of ideals of democracy and brotherhood is essential to a democratic state. But religion or religious institutions as political sovereigns defeat the purposes for which they exist. At the time of the writing of the Declaration of Independence and of the Constitution, nearly the whole Occidental world consisted of nations whose governments were based on the theory of divine right to rule. This theory was as great a distortion of religion as in modern days Nazi theories were distortions of religion.

Thomas Jefferson summed up the matter well in a letter to the Danbury Baptist Association in 1802. He wrote:

Believing with you, that religion is a matter which lies solely between man and his God, that he owes account to none for his faith or his worship, that the legislative powers of government reach action only, and not opinions, I contemplate with sovereign reverence that act of the whole American people which declared that their Legislature should "make no law respecting an establishment of religion or prohibiting the free exercise thereof," thus building a wall of separation between Church and State. Adhering to this expression of the supreme will of the nation in behalf of the rights of conscience, I shall see with sincere satisfaction the progress of those sentiments which tend to restore to man all his natural rights, convinced that he has no natural right in opposition to his social duties.

The quotations from the Presidents help to show how the unique American approach to religion has worked out. The reader will see, from the words of the men representing the beliefs of the American people, that religion has abided in our hearts, has been a dominant influence in our development as a nation, and at the same time has been kept free from the great distortion which brings destruction and degradation.

Can Belief in the Theory of "a Chosen People" and a God-Inspired "National Destiny" be Squared with the Ideals of Universal Brotherhood?

There are some who, upon reading what I have written, will agree, with one strong reservation. They will say it is all true, provided religion means nothing more than a belief in some vague, cloudy, distant Figure who in some remote way operates the universe without actually taking charge of anything directly concerning us.

[14]

If religion, however, they will add, means more than this —if it means a belief that God is our Creator and our Ruler, that He guides our steps, that He chooses certain peoples upon whom He showers unusual bounties and for whom He plans a special destiny of leadership—then have we not arrived at almost the same distortions which the United States was born to oppose and which do not square with ideals of universal brotherhood and equal rights for all?

This, it seems to me, is a reasonable question, which every individual should face and answer in his own way. I think it one of the most important questions in the world today, and I believe that the statements of the Presidents quoted here suggest an answer that is tremendously reassuring.

First of all, the epoch-making experiment in self-government begun by the United States nearly a century and three quarters ago was far from a simple and uncomplicated solution of the world's problems. It was fraught with immediate peril and also with long-range dangers, among the greatest of which have been those concerned with the unique American approach to religion and the simultaneous faith in God and His power.

Our history is both the history of an experiment in self-government and the history of a new concept of religion and its place in the lives of human beings.

We have survived the dangers, but we have not eliminated them, and I suppose they will always exist, bringing to mind the maxim that eternal vigilance is the price of liberty. Two of these dangers are always before us.

The first is that religion, whether a part of the state or

[15]

separated from it, may be used as what has been called "the opium of the people," in just the way that bread and circuses or strong drink can be so used, to hide deficiencies in justice and freedom and to beguile citizens from insisting upon their rights. Fortunately, the nature of the American experiment has made this danger almost negligible in our domestic development. In other countries this danger has been far from negligible, with a consequent impact on us and our foreign relations. Excesses in many nations have paved the way to what I must call the delusion among Communists that religion itself must be abolished to avert the danger, and the delusion is responsible for much of the international bitterness and trouble in the present period of history.

The second danger has threatened our country on numerous occasions. It is that even with the safeguard of separation of Church and State, belief in God and His apparent choice of certain peoples at certain times to act as leaders in human progress can intoxicate those peoples into disastrous confusion about their destiny. They come to believe that they are more than temporary leaders in human betterment; that instead, they have been divinely empowered to rule other peoples because they are members of a master nation or race.

This folly is what occurred in Germany, in Italy and in Japan. With variations of language, this folly is popular today in other nations. And hard as it may be for some readers to believe, it is a folly that has endangered the United States too during our history, sometimes bringing us to the brink of calamity.

[16]

Is Ours a Land of Destiny?

Because of the importance of this danger, I shall cite a specific example of the ease of falling into such folly, showing the unfortunate effect of the Spanish-American War of 1898 on many American minds. This effect can be seen in the following words from an address given in the Senate of the United States on January 9, 1900 by the then young and celebrated orator and Senator from Indiana, Albert J. Beveridge. I am indebted to that stirring work, *Our Times: The Turn of the Century*, by Mark Sullivan, for this and the succeeding quotation.

We will not renounce our part in the mission of the race, trustee, under God, of the civilization of the world . . . self-government and internal development have been the dominant notes of our first century; administration and the development of other lands will be the dominant notes of our second century. . . . He has made us [our race] the master organizers of the world to establish system where chaos reigns. . . . He has made us adepts in government that we may administer government among savage and senile peoples. . . . And of all our race, He has marked the American people as His chosen Nation to finally lead in the regeneration of the world. This is the divine mission of America, and it holds for us all the profit, all the glory, all the happiness possible to man. . . . The judgment of the Master is upon us: "Ye have been faithful over a few things; I will make you ruler over many things."

That these were not just the wild mouthings of an impassioned young orator is shown by the fact that at about the same time (ten months before, to be more precise) the well-known editor, William Allen White, had written in his *Emporia Gazette*, famed for its common-sense editorials:

[17]

It is the Anglo-Saxon's manifest destiny to go forth as a world conqueror. He will take possession of the islands of the sea. . . . This is what fate holds for the chosen people. It is so written. . . . It is to be.

Needless to say, the ideas were not adopted by the nation, and we were spared the calamity that would have been inevitable from such thinking.

I believe that the quotations from the Presidents illustrate the fact that the Presidents and the majority of the American people have always been aware of those dangers. They illustrate, too, what seems to me the basic fact about our faith in God's power and our destiny—that He has blessed us with the opportunity to provide abundance for ourselves, all of us, and to share the abundance with the world; that our destiny is to hold high the flaming torch of liberty for all, and to rule over none.

I know no finer expression of this than the words of Franklin Roosevelt less than six months before his death:

The creed of our democracy is that liberty is acquired and kept by men and women who are strong and self-reliant and possessors of such wisdom as God gives them—men and women who are just, and understanding, and generous to others—men and women who are capable of disciplining themselves.

For they are the rulers and they must rule themselves.

In this faith the people of the United States go forward under God.

II. OUR PEOPLE UNDER GOD

1. INTRODUCTION

THIS IS AN ACCOUNT of the lives of three hundred million men, women and children, who have made up the population of the United States from its inception to the present.

About half of them are alive today; the rest have passed on year by year. The reader may be as surprised to learn this startling fact as I was when the United States Census Bureau gave me this estimate. To realize that half of all the Americans who ever lived are still an active part of our nation is deeply thought-provoking.

These three hundred million have composed and built the first international nation in history, the first country whose people's origins and horizons have reached beyond its borders to every corner of our planet. They include those men and women about whom the most eloquent passages in our history have been written, that they "brought forth on this continent a new nation, conceived in liberty and dedicated to the proposition that all men are created equal." They include those descendants who underwent a war "testing whether that nation or any nation so conceived and so dedicated can long endure."

They include you and me and the rest of the living, more than ever intent on our resolve "that this nation, under God, shall have a new birth of freedom, and that government of the people, by the people, for the people, shall not perish from the earth."

I am not interested in "proving" that there is a God, or that God through a series of miraculous suspensions of, or interventions with, His normal laws of nature has shown special benefits to the American people.

The themes of this historical sketch are three. The first is that religious men and women, whether or not they had any formal creed, have been from the first days through to the present time almost entirely responsible for defiance of materialism, of age-old class distinctions of ancient beliefs in divinely given rights to special groups to rule other groups; and for an affirmative, working belief in the brotherhood and mutual responsibilities of man. These defiances and beliefs have made for an abundant life for a greater portion of the nation's inhabitants than has ever been the case in the world before.

The second theme is that, from the beginning, the weaker side—weaker in numbers and in physical and economic power, but backed by faith and religion—has consistently, though not always quickly, won against the stronger side in its struggles. It has won to such an extent that these victories are the real history of the United States.

This David-and-Goliath aspect of our national life, marked not by brief conflicts between two individuals but instead by movements that have swept the whole nation, has prevailed in other countries also, but it has been present more frequently and more consistently here than in any other nation, past or present. Sometimes this weaker side has won by evolution, sometimes by revolution, but generally the change has been by a peaceful process.

There is a third theme and a more important one which runs from the beginning to the end of this book. It is reflected in many of the quotations I have made from the Presidents. That theme is that this government of ours is set up for an ultimate purpose even greater and more important than those current purposes for which America apparently exists today. The theme is expressed so strongly that it becomes clear that we American people must never think that this land is ours in the sense that we can mutilate it and shamefully use it and live thoughtlessly as though we do not respect America's meaning and destiny.

If my themes and interpretations are valid, the history of the American people may well be termed the most profound acknowledgment of the goodness and power of God that has ever been known. More than this, it may be called the greatest acknowledgment of the direction in which God is leading mankind that has ever been known. This is important, for throughout the world today there are hundreds of millions of people who are daily being instructed by teachers to whom religion and the concept of God has understandably but erroneously become an abomination.

I use the word "understandably," because the distortions of religion which have been practiced and in some places are today practiced—the misuse of religion and the concept of God as instruments of terror, torture, hatred, tyranny and totalitarianism, and as support of the crumbling edifices of ignorance and superstition—are horrible enough to embitter almost any unthinking person and to make him lose faith, turning from God without comprehending that he should turn only from the distortions. And I use the word "erroneously," because when we turn from God, there is nothing constructive left, and we follow a road which inevitably leads to the same conditions that originally outraged us.

Long and complex as our history is, it can be comprised within the lifetime of as few as three individuals. For example, Charles Evans Hughes, who died in 1948, was born in the year that John Tyler died; and Tyler was born in the year that Benjamin Franklin died; and Franklin was born in 1706, when the English colonies were just beginning to take permanent shape.

For the purpose of this sketch, I have selected four Presidents whose lives covered the whole span of our history as a nation, up to 1945: Thomas Jefferson, 1743-1826; Abraham Lincoln, 1809-1865; Woodrow Wilson, 1856-1924; and Franklin Roosevelt, 1882-1945. I do not present biographies of these men, but instead sketch some aspects of the world in which each of them was born, grew up and died; the impact of that world on them; and what seems to me the essential part each played in the life of the American people. This is preceded by a description of pre-United States years in North America.

2. THE PRE-UNITED STATES WORLD OF NORTH AMERICA

ON THE PURELY natural plane, two predominant features distinguish human beings, animals and plant life from one another. These are their relative powers of independent movement and their relative abilities to alter their environment. Plant life has almost no power of independent movement from one site to another and therefore almost no opportunity to change its environment. Animal life does possess the power of independent movement and this enormous difference enables individual beings to change one environment for another, to seek the most appropriate spots for food, shelter and other necessities.

But man, in addition to the power of independent movement, possesses not only the ability to move from one environment to another but also the ability to alter the environment in which he is—to bring heat and light where there are cold and darkness, to hew down trees and create homes, and to execute the million other environmental alterations that make up the activities of mankind.

When we look back on American history, a strong temptation arises to believe the rather florid and largely mythical story many of us were taught in our childhood, that

[25]

the New World which Christopher Columbus unknowingly discovered was a vast storehouse of treasure and natural resources which needed only the coming of Europeans to cause it to pour forth its bounties. In other words, all that was needed, according to the story, for Europeans to possess this storehouse of all human delights, was for them to exercise their power of independent movement by sailing across the Atlantic. It is true that in parts of South America and in Mexico large accumulations of gold and treasure were "confiscated" from the native owners, and that their mines were exploited, but this was a temporary and quickly exhausted source. This fact did not deter explorers from promulgating the story of fabulous and inexhaustible riches.

Indeed, for about 150 years after Columbus' epochal trip, so many explorers and emissaries from the royal courts of Europe issued glowing reports of this type that it came to be second nature to believe the story. And nowadays, when that portion of the New World which became the United States is the most prosperous and physically powerful nation on earth, there seems to be confirmation for it.

The facts are, however, quite different. The so-called New World was no newer than the rest of the world and had been created at precisely the same time. To speak of its "discovery" means actually that a relatively small segment of the world's people, those living in Great Britain and certain European countries, became aware of its existence. Many centuries before Columbus, even many centuries before the Vikings of Iceland made their journeys to the New World, human beings had exercised their power of independent movement to inhabit the New World and had not found this power conducive in any large measure to any more abundant life than could be found elsewhere.

An even more impressive fact is that these inhabitants, as they spread over the immense areas of what later came to be called North America and South America, and over the various islands that bordered the shores of these two continents, found that the area which now comprises the United States was the least attractive, the least valuable, and the least tolerable of any they knew, except for some of the far northern areas of what are now Canada and Alaska.

This is attested to by the population groupings in the New World when Europeans began their explorations. The inhabitants of what is now the United States were a few hundred thousand, scattered among a number of tribes who lived, with some exceptions, in conditions of want, malnutrition, ill-health and endless forays to steal food from one another. But at the same time, what are now Mexico, South America and the islands of the Atlantic, contained millions of inhabitants, many living in nations of relative prosperity and abundance.

Historians estimate that the small Island of Hispaniola, now comprising Haiti and the Dominican Republic, at the time Columbus arrived, contained anywhere from several hundred thousand to several million inhabitants. When it is recalled that nearly two hundred years later, as the United States Government began to function under the Constitution in 1790, the whole United States contained less than four million, the story of the vast storehouse of treasure which only awaited man's exercise of his power for independent motion in order for him to possess it falls to the ground.

The real story of the American people is, therefore, largely one of man's exercise of his power to alter his environment. Without denying in any way the vast natural resources of our nation, its fertility and its grandeur, we can still explode the myth of plain luck and good fortune in the building of our country. There are vast stretches of the earth, near and far, which today possess and have always possessed as many natural resources as the United States. They too have blossomed or will blossom when their inhabitants have been or will be moved by faith, by determination and by their God-given ingenuity to alter their environments in order to provide abundance.

Because the exercise of man's power to alter his environment involves struggle against the elements and sometimes among human beings, the real story of the American people is one of a series of struggles. The greater number of these struggles have been what might almost be termed hopeless, because the odds were apparently insuperable. This characteristic of the struggles raises the plane of action from the purely natural to the spiritual. By spiritual I mean that those qualities of the spirit transcending a mere desire to continue existence or to make it more comfortable have been the mainsprings of our nation's achievements.

The pre-United States world of North America can roughly be said to have existed between the years 1607 and 1740. Much that happened before 1607 had a direct bearing on the development of that world, and the United States seemed far from a nation in 1740. But during that period occurred the struggles and events which formed the foundation for our country.

The first of the struggles was that of getting safely over the Atlantic Ocean from British and European ports. To embark on these voyages meant literally to take one's life in one's hands. For explorers and adventurers in search of gold and treasure such voyages are easy to understand, as their careers depended on taking enormous gambles with fate. And that slaves and semislaves made the voyages in preference to immediate death is also understandable, for they had little choice. But that men and women and whole families who were farmers or tradesmen or mechanics should voluntarily make the perilous voyage, not for treasure but to find a new place to live, seems almost incomprehensible in today's world.

And added to the wonder at the spirit that animated the immigrants is the wonder that so many arrived safely. The art of navigation was well advanced, but the relative tininess of the sailing ships, the slow speed of the voyage, requiring food and water to last for many months, the storm areas of the Atlantic stretching from Hatteras down across the Caribbean Sea—all combined to form barriers which inevitably resulted in much loss of life. Yet enough did arrive safely to build gradually a population, over a century and a quarter, of over a million people.

The next struggle was that of developing communities and homes after arrival, and in the earlier years this was so acute that it dwarfed the dangers of making the Atlantic crossing. Here came the initial application of the power to alter one's environment, and to succeed seemed beyond human endurance. For a great many years, the struggle for physical survival was a dominating force. The narrow strip of land bordering the Atlantic coast had to be the main source of food, shelter and clothing, and all three of these required alteration of the environment. The climate in many areas struck men dead with its fierce cold and winds, and in other areas men were enervated with its intense heat. The Indian tribes, naturally resentful of the intrusion of strangers in their world, and of the various attempts to rob, extirpate, oust, torture and enslave them, continually menaced the lives and safety of the new inhabitants.

As time went by, the struggle for survival passed the critical stage. Even before that, other and more far-reaching struggles had begun. Clearly, if the colonists had not survived, there would be no United States today; but it is equally true that if they had survived physically and yet had not fought out the other struggles, there would be no United States as we know it today.

The gradual infiltration of the Atlantic coast by British and European citizens represented four distinct and basic social, economic and political movements which necessarily conflicted with one another. First, there was the movement to establish a colonial empire along the lines of age-old empires of the past (and of some empires that linger to the present day). Second, there was the movement to import the civilization of the European world into the New World. Third, there was the movement to escape the civilization of the European world. Finally, there was the movement to create a new civilization.

In all exterior considerations, the last movement was the weakest. It had little financial and legal backing. Its proponents were in a minority, and were often confused about their own aims. History, tradition, patriotic concepts of the time, even many religious concepts of the day, all pointed to failure. That it succeeded in as large a measure as it did was, to my mind, miraculous and evidence of God's hand in the affairs of men. I do not say that it succeeded completely, for many of the issues of the struggles were not settled for a great many years thereafter, and some of them have not been entirely settled today. But it succeeded in large enough measure to mark a new epoch in the history of mankind.

The first movement, that of establishing a colonial empire, had one vital defect, in so far as the territory now comprising the United States was concerned. The *sine qua non* of a colonial empire is the possession of great numbers of primitive natives who can be forced into a state of slavery or semislavery, and made to do the physical work necessary to exploit the riches of the empire for the benefit of the new masters. Much to the vexation of the empire builders, this *sine qua non* was missing.

There were relatively few Indians, and though arduous efforts were made by the empire builders to force them into slavery, the Indians did not approve and failed to lend themselves to this purpose. Indeed, they were so obtuse that instead of spending twenty hours a day tilling a field or doing some other backbreaking work for the new masters, they were likely to scalp them and burn their houses down. Little as they had done in the past to develop the resources of the New World, they seemed to have caught some of its spirit of independence. I wonder if the white settlers did not increase their own ideas of liberty from the examples set by the savages.

A scheme was thought out to solve the problem. Why not import the necessary population group of slaves? It had been discovered in this period that Africa abounded in apparently suitable prospects. Expeditions were therefore organized to capture these Africans, throw them into ships, bring them across the Atlantic, and then hold them in slavery, if they were still in fit condition to work, which could readily be determined by testing their ability to live under harsh and often brutal treatment.

It is saddening to have to report that this scheme worked out with considerable success in certain parts of the pre-United States world of North America and led to conditions and problems which, to some extent, are still with us. The comparative success of the movement can be determined by the fact that at the time of the founding of the United States, Negro slaves represented between 10 and 15 per cent of the whole population, which is approximately the same percentage as that of Negroes today.

Yet, even in the period we are considering, the colonial empire movement was beginning to fail. For one thing, a thriving colonial empire requires that the slave population be not 10 or 15 per cent of the total population, but 90 per cent or more. A fraction of the 10 per cent remaining are the owners of the slaves, lands and plantations, and the rest are overseers, managers and other salaried employees of the owners. Considerable capital is required to be an owner of this kind of enterprise, particularly when the slaves have to be imported from another continent. This was far beyond the capacity of all but a few of the European colonists, and most of them had to make their living in humbler ways than empire building. Their presence inevitably tended to uproot and interfere with the colonial empire movement. Even in the areas in which slaves were most heavily concentrated, from 30 to 50 per cent of the population were free Europeans or indentured workers who could obtain freedom by a series of years of work.

The second movement was to import European civilization to the New World. This differed from the empire movement in that it consisted of efforts to duplicate European, chiefly British, political, social and economic patterns. Over the years, place names reflected this movement, with the prefix "New" to such areas as Amsterdam, York, Hampshire, Jersey, London, England and the like.

The whole structure of European civilization was founded on the universal acceptance of the theory of the divine right of kings. Temporal power was believed to flow directly from God to certain individuals and their immediate families, and through them to a larger group of individuals who formed the nobility or aristocracy. The people generally might have attained what was called freedom in certain individual pursuits, but fundamentally they were "subjects" of whatever king or queen happened to be ruling, instead of being what are today called citizens. Taxes were collected not for the common good, but for the coffers of the king, who might in his wisdom devote part of his money for the benefit of his subjects.

[33]

I know no more graphic illustration of this concept than the "Epistle Dedicatory" to the King James translation of the Bible, issued by its translators in 1611, four years after the settlement of Jamestown, Virginia, and eleven years before the landing of the Pilgrims at Plymouth. They were so much imbued by the concept of the divine right of kings, or so much scared by it, that they felt compelled to pen their extraordinary dedication, addressed "To the most high and mighty Prince James, by the grace of God, King of Great Britain, France and Ireland, Defender of the Faith, &c."

The following excerpt from the dedication gives a clear idea of the divine-right theory:

"Great and manifold were the blessings, most dread Sovereign, which Almighty God, the Father of all mercies, bestowed upon us the people of *England,* when first he sent Your Majesty's Royal Person to rule and reign over us . . . the appearance of Your Majesty, as the *Sun* in his strength . . . gave unto all that were well affected exceeding cause of comfort; especially when we beheld the Government established in Your Highness, and Your hopeful Seed. . . .

"Your very name is precious among them [the English people]: their eye doth behold You with comfort, and they bless You in their hearts, as that sanctified Person, who, under God, is the immediate Author of their true happiness . . . we hold it our duty to offer it to Your Majesty, not only as our King and Sovereign, but as to the principal Mover and Author of the work. . . . The Lord of heaven and earth bless Your Majesty with many and happy days, that, as his heavenly hand hath enriched Your Highness with many singular and extraordinary graces, so You may be the wonder of the world in this latter age for happiness and true felicity . . ."

[34]

The movement to import European civilization to North America was based on these same concepts. From the founding of Jamestown in 1607 through 1732, when Georgia was settled, thirteen British colonies were gradually formed or absorbed from settlements by the French, Dutch, Swedish and other colonists. Each of the colonies was separate in government, but all adhered to the British crown. Government varied in the colonies and democratic processes had reached proportions which made a complete break not alone with England but with the whole divine-right theory inevitable, though few colonists realized it at the time. The old forms were still in operation. There were the charter colonies, existing under contract with the king; the proprietary colonies, governed by a so-called proprietor who had been "given" the colonies by the king; and the crown colonies, with governors appointed directly by the king.

This movement was instrumental in preventing the colonial empire movement from attaining full success, for whatever defects it had, the status of the people was different from that of slaves, and their presence in large numbers forced the germinating nation further and further from a colonial type of existence.

In turn, the movement in its original form was itself brought to failure by the third and fourth movements of that epochal period. The third movement was the antithesis of the second. It was the movement, not to import, but to escape from, European civilization. From the time of the very first settlements, emigrants from England and other countries were in large majority men and women dominated by the idea of leaving behind them once and for all conditions which they had found almost unbearable.

There were many individual motives for making the hazardous journey across the Atlantic, but three predominated. One was to escape from religious persecution; another was to escape from the rigors of laws of the time; another was to escape from conditions of unemployment, poverty and destitution.

During this entire period, England and most of Europe were undergoing vast changes in religious belief. New Christian denominations and sects were spreading. Tied in with the theory of the divine right of kings was a concept in which the Church and the State formed one integral unit. Each nation had its official religion, and the king was its temporal head. In nearly all countries it was obligatory to belong to the official church or to suffer penalties ranging from ostracism to execution. To embrace another religious belief was to become immediately involved in persecution.

Thus it happened that many of the settlements in North America came into being because of the desire to escape religious persecution. Catholics, Protestants and Jews alike saw in the New World an opportunity to practice their faiths in peace, and they seized this opportunity in increasing numbers. Many of us are under the impression that this motive was prominent only at the beginning of colonization, but the fact is that it continued to be prominent throughout the entire period from 1607 to 1740 and far beyond it.

To a lesser degree, other Europeans found the oppression of secular laws intolerable. Restrictions on personal movement from place to place, the continual menace of impressment into military service, ruinously high taxes, inability to alter one's occupation or status, and many similar conditions filled thousands of people with a desire for escape from a life that seemed one of bondage.

Finally, the fifteenth and sixteenth centuries in Europe were characterized by unemployment and destitution on a tremendous scale. After the endings of wars, soldiers found themselves homeless and unable to get employment. Changes in agricultural practices, particularly in England, resulted in wholesale ejection of farm workers from their former toil, with no way of making a living. To many of these people, the New World offered escape from the threat of starvation. The trading companies that were operating settlements in America were constantly seeking workers. They offered to pay passage across the Atlantic in exchange for agreements to "work the debt out" over a term of years, and these "indentured servants" came to form a large population group in the colonies. Others were able to pay their own passage by selling their possessions and so were free at once, but the motive of escape from economic distress was the same.

The fourth movement in the colonial world of North America, as I have said above, was the weakest in its beginnings. It was also entirely unplanned. While its origins lay in concepts of liberty and government that originated in Europe and Asia, the movement itself became a reality only with the impact of the New World on its new inhabitants.

This movement was to create a new civilization which would depart basically from any civilization before known.

[37]

It would establish an entirely new concept of inherent rights of individuals and their relationships to one another and to their government. It would overthrow the whole concept of the divine right of kings or anyone else to rule others. It would irrevocably separate Church and State.

To tell in detail how this was accomplished, or to what extent it was accomplished, is beyond the province of this work. In reference to the period from 1607 to 1740, I merely want to point out a number of the principal factors that shaped the movement to create a new civilization, for they established the basis on which the nation of the future was to be built.

As important as any other factor was the building of a new attitude toward human labor. To put the matter baldly, during most of the world's recorded history it has been taught that a state of idleness is one of the supreme achievements of life; and even today millions of people still so consider it. The whole theory of aristocracy stems from the idea that work is distasteful, degrading and dishonorable. Heaven in the minds of many inhabitants of the world has always been pictured as a place in which the angels do nothing except enjoy themselves, and work to them has never been associated with enjoyment. So completely were such beliefs held in bygone ages that many aristocrats considered even the labor of learning to read and write below their dignity, and relegated such things to the clergy and other more humble folk. Aristotle could not conceive of a state without slaves.

The presence in the New World of hosts of slaves and indentured servants was testimony to the popularity of this attitude. But the great majority of the colonists had to work to live, and the work was largely done not for masters, but for themselves. Work, labor, toil, call it what you will, came to be something worth doing, something that was dignified and honorable.

A man might be poor or rich, but he was taught that work, not idleness, was a virtue. This was one of the most revolutionary changes of all time. The practice of work was far more powerful than philosophical speculation in weaving the pattern of democracy. And during the century and a quarter of this period a fundamental sense of equality that came from work with others on an equal basis became a foundation stone for the United States.

It is hardly necessary to point out the strong influence of religion in this change in attitude toward human labor. The tenets of all the religious denominations represented in the colonies included this attitude toward work, as they always had. Now those tenets became a matter of practice rather than of pious teaching, which religious instructors had usually applied only to the "lower" classes. The religious men and women of the colonies simply found themselves with the opportunity—indeed, the necessity—to carry out their faith in their daily lives. Their religion gave them the courage to do work and the understanding to give to work a status of dignity. Not only was the laborer considered worthy of his hire. The man or woman who did not work was considered unworthy of his obligations and privileges.

Allied with this attitude toward work was another factor, the new-found opportunity for human beings to exercise choice in their occupations and in the places in which they lived. In England, as in all Europe, men's lives were to a great extent cast in molds. From childhood to death, their occupation was fixed for them, with little chance of change. Also there were relatively few geographical changes of homes, except when desperation or hunger drove people to new areas. In some ways, conditions were similar in the New World at first, but this quickly changed. Benjamin Franklin, born in 1706, was an excellent example of the way human beings could exercise choice in their occupations and in their geographical locations. But even Franklin had to run away to be free. And when he did, his breaking of an apprenticeship bond showed the force of old custom, because Franklin wrote of the offense as if it were on his conscience. But there was a virgin continent at each man's back door, and the desire to better one's conditions by pushing westward was increasingly strong, so that the whole period was one of constant movement and expansion.

A third factor in the movement to create a new civilization was the entirely new experience of the colonists in finding it necessary to meet the problems of what may be called multidenominational religious expression. The colonists who came to America to escape religious persecution did not have in mind at all what is today called freedom of religion. Each group wanted to end the dangers and suffering of being a religious minority group, and felt that by going to the New World, it could establish a community in which it was the majority group. Religious persecution commenced in the New World almost the moment the religious groups began arriving, and flourished during the whole of the colonial period.

But it also began weakening almost as soon as it began rising.

While a particular colony or community might have an official church and persecute all nonbelievers, there was too much interchange among inhabitants of colonies, too much immigration of new colonists of differing faiths, too much conversion of individuals and families from one faith to another, too much migration to new communities, for there ever to develop a continental state religion or even a single majority group. Nothing like this had ever happened before, and the colonists were compelled by these circumstances to develop a pattern of life in which numerous denominations existed side by side.

Through these experiences, the concept of religious freedom and, to a large extent, the concept of separation of Church and State, became realities, and were increasingly practiced.

Religion also was instrumental in initiating and developing another great institution, that of public education. In most of the religious denominations literacy was necessary for such practices as reading the Bible and understanding sermons and religious literature. Not only did ministers have to be trained, but all members had to have some education. In this way, the concept of the advisability of widespread instruction came into being, and with it, as time passed, the concept of education for other than purely religious purposes. By 1740 public education had come to have a firm hold in many of the colonies, though it was still largely in its infancy.

Still another factor was important during this period.

[41]

Even though government was under the direction of the British crown, it was not feasible to create local and community units of government of the old style, so that self-government developed with amazing strides. Men learned how to vote, despite many limitations; how to choose public officials from a restricted few; how to exercise their power in building and aiding their communities; and thus they laid a foundation for the state governments to come and the national government that was unconsciously being created.

These and many other circumstances all contributed to a gradual overthrow of social and economic barriers as they had existed in the Old World. Most of these great and revolutionary changes were wrought in the century and a quarter that ended in 1740. There was not yet unity, not yet a crystallization of the changes into concrete forms. But the foundations had been firmly made. Three years later, on April 13, 1743, Thomas Jefferson was born, and we shall next look at the world in which he grew up, lived and died.

3. THE WORLD OF THOMAS JEFFERSON
1743-1826

THE PERIOD OF AMERICAN HISTORY which we have just surveyed is probably the least known to most Americans. In
the minds of many boys and girls at school, it might aptly
be termed the hop, skip and jump period. The hop is Columbus' voyage across the Atlantic; then one skips to the landings at Jamestown and Plymouth; and finally one jumps to
the dramatic days of, "But as for me, give me liberty or give
me death."

Conversely, most of the period in which Thomas Jefferson lived is by far the best-known of all. A boy or girl who
may stumble and look blank when asked about William
Bradford or John Harvard or Anne Bradstreet, can be glib,
vivid and informative regarding Aaron Burr, Paul Revere
or Betsy Ross. So great is the emphasis on this portion of
our nation's life that it often surpasses not only the remoter
past but also more recent periods. The same boy or girl can
conceivably tell more about James Madison or Thomas
Paine in five minutes than he can relate in half an hour
about such figures as Herbert Hoover or William Jennings
Bryan, although the latter have influenced the lives of perhaps forty times as many million people.

Many reasons for this emphasis are obvious. Two are less so, and because they are intimately associated with the purposes and themes of this sketch, I shall mention them.

Few, if any, periods in recorded history produced a larger number of human figures touched by eternal greatness than did this. Perhaps from this distance we have cast them in more heroic molds than they really filled, but even discounting the veneration which time builds, the period was thronged with many of the really great men of world history. When the extremely small population of the budding nation (less than four million in 1790) is taken into account, the marvel of it is even greater. I have said that I am not interested in trying to interpret God's handiwork in the United States in terms of individual miracles, but if that were my purpose, I know no better case that could be made for such an interpretation than the appearance in a tiny set of colonies with a large population group of slaves and semislaves, of a host of men of genius, profundity, strength, talent and an indomitable spirit of independence and brotherhood.

Many thinkers have asserted that this "golden age" in American history actually resulted from the direct interposition of Divine Providence, which caused great leaders to be born and to build the colonies into a nation. Without any inclination to dispute this view, my thesis differs. In the preceding section I have attempted to paint briefly the picture of a whole civilization in the process of being created, not by means of formidable leaders but by the impact of the New World on hundreds of thousands of men, women and children.

In this connection, a statement of John Adams, quoted by Oscar R. Straus in *The Origin of Republican Form of Government*, is interesting:

Independence of State and Church was the fundamental principle of the first colonists, has been its general principle for two hundred years, and now we hope is past dispute. Who, then, was the author, inventor, discoverer of Independence? The only true answer must be, the first emigrants; and the proof of it is the charter of James the I. When we say that Otis, Adams, Mayhew, Henry, Lee, Jefferson, etc., were authors of independence, we ought to say they were only awakeners and revivers of the original fundamental principle of colonization.

This impact on the people themselves gave release for the first time to many of the colonists' religious impulses, a challenge to their ingenuity and courage, the necessity for overthrowing traditional political, economic and social patterns, and a desire for a new kind of human relationship. To my mind, it was an inevitable consequence that religious people engaged in seemingly hopeless struggles and won them. Another inevitable consequence was that an atmosphere came into being which almost automatically brought forth great leaders. As I have pointed out before, this to me is the greatest tribute to God and His power in the affairs of men that the history of our nation offers, or could possibly offer.

The second less obvious reason for emphasis on this historical period is that much of its significance lay in military and political developments in crystallized form, like the writing of the Declaration of Independence, the winning of the Revolution and of the War of 1812, the writing and ratification of the Constitution, the establishment of the national government, and so on. Such things are dramatic, and incidentally easier to remember than the continuing struggles of a whole people.

Here again an excellent case could be made, and has often been made, for the claim that Divine Providence intervened directly in the affairs of the budding nation, in hundreds of instances in which natural laws were apparently suspended. I shall not deny the validity of this interpretation, but shall continue to maintain my thesis that all these great events were the inevitable climaxes of the choices made by a whole people largely infiltrated with religious faith and reliance on the Lord, not for miracles but instead for strength.

That spirit was unforgettably demonstrated in 1775 when Ethan Allen and his eighty-three Green Mountain Boys attacked Fort Ticonderoga, demanding the fort's surrender. When questioned in whose name surrender was asked, Allen thundered: "In the name of the Great Jehovah and the Continental Congress!" They were fighting for God, not just God for them.

It is necessary, therefore, to see this period as one in the life of a whole and growing people creating an entirely new civilization. It is necessary to understand the full implications of Emerson's immortal lines,

> Here once the embattled farmers stood
> And fired the shot heard 'round the world.

In the same way, each individual must be seen as a whole human being rather than as a figure participating in one or two or three great incidents of history. In the world of Thomas Jefferson, which lasted from 1743 to 1826, a period of eighty-three years, Jefferson was always the same person with the same immortal soul—as a little boy, as a justice of the peace, as President of the United States, as the purchaser of that vast area in the south and west known as the Louisiana Purchase territory, as the compiler of what is known as the Jefferson Bible, and as an aging man corresponding regularly and affectionately with his old opponent, John Adams, who died on the same day as Jefferson.

When Jefferson was born, Benjamin Franklin was thirty-seven years old. As I have said, the foundations of our national government had been laid, but none was aware of the fact. Yet the distinctively American characteristics of the people had been created and were spreading throughout the colonies. There were perhaps a million people in the thirteen colonies at that time, and Georgia had not yet been officially chartered as a colony, though it had been settled nine years before. The colonists occupied a thin strip of land along the Atlantic coast.

When Jefferson died, he left behind him a nation of twenty-four States and about eleven million inhabitants, stretching from Maine to the border of Florida and irregularly more than halfway westward across the North American continent; within another quarter century the entire continent north of Mexico and south of Canada was to be occupied by states and territories. The nation had not only won independence from England in a long war, but had retained it in another, and had also won independence from all of Europe. It stood on its own feet as self-sufficient,

[47]

sovereign, ready to protect itself from all attacks and to protect its neighboring nations of the New World from European inroads.

That this represented something infinitely more important than the mere rise of a new nation, something basically different from what had been known in the world before, is attested to by the reactions of European government leaders. Successively their attitudes developed from faint amusement at the audacity of the ignorant colonists, to annoyance, to alarm, to fury, and finally almost to terror.

The Declaration of the Holy Alliance in 1815 stated:

The high contracting parties, well convinced that the system of representative government is as incompatible with the monarchical principle as the maxim of the sovereignty of the people is opposed to the principle of the divine right, engage in the most solemn manner to employ all their means and unite all their efforts to put an end to the system of representative government, wherever it is known to exist in the States of Europe, and to prevent its being introduced into those states where it is not known.

Three years before Jefferson died, the Monroe Doctrine was promulgated. Metternich, in a violent protest, wrote:

The United States, which we have seen arise and grow . . . have suddenly left a sphere too narrow for their ambition, and have astonished Europe by a new act of revolt. . . . They have distinctly and clearly announced their intention to set not only power against power, but, to express it more exactly, altar against altar. In their indecent declarations they have cast blame and scorn on the institutions of Europe most worthy of respect. . . . In permitting themselves these unprovoked attacks, in fostering revolutions wherever they show themselves, in regretting those which have failed, in extending a helping hand to those which seem to prosper, they lend new strength to the apostles of sedition, and reanimate the courage of every conspirator. If this flood of evil doctrines and pernicious examples should extend over the whole of Europe, what would become of our religious and political institutions, of the moral force of our governments, and of that conservative system which has saved Europe from dissolution?

What the European government leaders missed completely in their observation of developments was that political and military actions, declarations, doctrines and constitutions meant nothing in themselves beyond heroic personal achievements and excellent flights of eloquence, and that what made them formidable and world-shaking was the day-by-day life of the people of the new nation. It was a new type of living beyond the comprehension of those whose minds were fettered by chains of tradition, whose religions and religious impulses had never been given the opportunity to become part of the daily scheme of living.

It is true that during the whole of this period in the United States the colonial empire movement flourished within certain limits; that the movement to import European civilization made headway; that a fairly large part of the American inhabitants lived in physical slavery, semi-slavery, and increasingly, economic bondage to the rising industrial empires; that the struggle for physical survival as the nation moved west remained grim and real. But the majority of the people were not in bondage. They were free and their own masters. And never before had this been true.

So, to understand what the European leaders could not grasp, we must see the activities of the American people as the real development of the nation, and the political triumphs and declarations as simply the expression in law and government of those activities in altering the environment in which the people lived.

The opening up of the great Northwest Territory in 1787 ranked in importance with the writing in the same year of the Constitution, and the acquiring of the immense areas of the Louisiana territory in 1803 with the establishment of a national government. Improvements in transportation by land and by water with the invention of steamships and the building of highways and canals, improvement in agricultural methods and startling new inventions in the field of agriculture and industry, were all in the forefront of the building of the nation.

All this involved struggles, many struggles. Most of them were, as before and later, struggles that seemed almost hopeless, with the weaker side slowly but surely winning in the long run. Here again the hand of God can be seen, giving strength when it is asked and making victory possible.

In the boyhood of Thomas Jefferson, the first of these struggles was taking place, the struggle for self-government in colony-wide units. As has been pointed out before, a measure of self-government in local units began in the 1600's and increased rapidly in some of the colonies, because of the difficulty of imposing outside rule in small communities. British officials did not have the necessary staffs for detailed supervision of the life of the colonists, and self-government began and grew largely by default. So by the time of Jefferson's birth, except in larger communities, the inhabitants of each community were ruling themselves to a very large extent.

The local systems were far from democratic from today's point of view, for religious, property and other restrictions rarely allowed a majority of the inhabitants of a community to have an active voice in affairs, but there was gradual development, which inevitably led to steps looking toward self-rule for a whole colony. It seemed impossible that this could ever be achieved, for here the British authorities had physical power to enforce their demands, but in spite of this, by the time Jefferson was eleven years old, the colonies were acting for themselves in a great many ways.

During these years, there were continuous conflicts between British and French settlers in North America, and in 1754 the British crown felt it desirable that the colonies form an alliance for fighting the French, and encouraged the calling of a conference to work out a plan. This was the celebrated Albany Conference engineered by Benjamin Franklin. The plan worked out by the delegates, however, was unsatisfactory to the colonists and to the king, as both felt it dangerously like a step toward a unified government for the colonies, which seemed to be universally opposed. This marked the beginning of a struggle immensely more difficult than that for self-rule for an individual colony, the struggle for a united government. That the main issues of this struggle were settled in a little more than twenty years is one of the most astonishing facts of this period.

The king of England and his advisers were probably as influential in creating the United States as any of the colonists, for England at this time commenced a series of actions of a tyrannical nature, actions which I shall not name, for they are brilliantly enumerated in the Declaration of Independence. In order not to surrender the way of life that had been built up for a century and a half, the colonists were finally almost literally forced to rebel against England, to unite with one another and to declare independence.

But this is only the negative side of the birth of our nation. It was one thing to declare independence from a tyrannical master, and to fight to the death, if need be, to establish this independence. It was another to devise a form of government to replace the former one, and here the new attitude toward life that had been developed over the years in America displayed itself in the expression of a unique concept.

The Declaration of Independence is really two documents. One of them gives the reasons why the rule of the colonies by England was intolerable and why independence was indispensable. The other states the basic features of a new kind of human government. It is much briefer than the first, containing only 456 words of the total of 1,338. Indeed, its essence—what might be termed the message carried by "the shot heard 'round the world"—totals only 182 words, which are worth repeating here, no matter how often they have been read before:

When, in the Course of human events, it becomes necessary for one people to dissolve the political bands which have connected them with another, and to assume among the powers of the earth, the separate and equal station to which the Laws of Nature and of Nature's God entitle them, a decent respect to the opinions of mankind requires that they should declare the causes which impel them to the separation.

We hold these truths to be self-evident, that all men are created equal, that they are endowed by their Creator with certain unalienable Rights, that among these are Life, Liberty and the pursuit of Happiness. That to secure these rights, Governments are instituted among Men, deriving their just powers from the consent of the governed. That whenever any Form of Government becomes destructive of these ends, it is the Right of the People to alter or to abolish it, and to institute new Government, laying its foundation on such principles and organizing its powers in such form, as to them shall seem most likely to effect their Safety and Happiness.

This statement explodes another largely mythical story which many of us were taught as children in school, similar to the story about the wealth of the New World when Columbus sailed the Atlantic. According to this story the colonists formed a government closely patterned after the republic of Rome and the so-called democracies of Greece. It is true that certain exterior features of government, like the parliamentary system, had some resemblance to those in ancient countries. But in the days of the glory that was Greece and the grandeur that was Rome, both Rome and Athens were fundamentally slave states in which democracy as we understand it was unheard-of. Plato's proposed "Republic" was no more like a republic as we envision it than was Hitler's Germany.

To the last man, every Athenian or old Roman would have been horrified by the statement just quoted from the Declaration of Independence regarding equality.

So astounding is it in its plain meaning that many Americans today have not yet found themselves able to accept or agree with it.

The mighty struggle to achieve independence and to create a new form of government was won by a minority of the colonists. Approximately a quarter of the inhabitants of the colonies were slaves or semislaves and naturally did not participate in the struggle; probably nearly all of them were unaware of it. Another 10 per cent, numbering when the Revolution began more than 200,000 people, firmly opposed it, and pledged their allegiance to England and the old ways of living. Another and still larger population group was busy with its own immediate concerns, in extending western frontiers and conducting its struggles for physical survival, so that it paid little attention to the war.

How, then, could the relatively small band of revolutionists have won a war against the mightiest military power on earth? With all due credit to the masterly tactics of Washington and the Continental Army, to Franklin in enlisting the aid of France, and to all the other direct and positive efforts by the colonists, the seemingly hopeless struggle was won because Goliath did not think the matter important enough to concentrate on wiping out his little defiant foe. England was immersed in weightier matters, like the endless game of chess played on the chessboard of Europe. And so, after eight years, peace was concluded, and England accepted the fact that a new nation existed.

It was tolerant about it, for it knew that when the opportunity arose later, it could swoop in and take back the territory it had lost. But when, in 1812, the opportunity arose, it was too late.

The Revolution sought to accomplish three ends. The first was independence from the rule of England. The second was the overthrow of the divine-right theory and system of government, with the substitution of the principles of the equality of all people in their rights and privileges and of the sovereignty of the people in government. The third was a working partnership among the thirteen former colonies. Only the first of these was fully accomplished. The other two were approached and a firm foundation was laid for their eventual accomplishment, but many a struggle lay ahead.

One of the most interesting phases of this whole period was that situations and relationships were created which required a new word in the English language to cope with them. Its spelling is identical with that of a much older word, but its meaning is basically different, and the differentiation was a gradual process over many years. The word is "State." The original meaning, still in use in appropriate context, is what we now call more frequently country or nation. The new meaning or word denotes a curious and novel type of subdivision of a nation, which is both subordinate to the nation and at the same time sovereign. When the colonies declared themselves free of England, they were obviously no longer colonies, but neither were they parts of a new country. They were nations in their own right, allied for various purposes. Yet the Declaration of Independence by its

[55]

very nature indicated that one nation, not thirteen, was announcing its establishment; and the Constitution made explicit what was only implied in the former document. Despite this, the name "United States of America," which was used formally for the first time in the Declaration of Independence, was used as a plural form, and the Constitution followed the same practice.

This commentary on the development of our nation from a group of colonies is also a commentary on the aspiration of the people to overthrow every vestige of the divine-right system of government. The people did not spend much time on theological and philosophical aspects of the divine-right theory. To them this theory meant kings and nobles and appointed officials and foreign soldiers, and government itself as they knew it. They eyed monarchical government with loathing, and all government with suspicion. Government meant literally governing, use of arbitrary authority, and all the traditions built up for a century and a half made them rebel.

Throughout our history, Americans have been known as the most resistant to authority of any people in the world, and this spirit was flowering. It coincided with the release of their religious impulses and their religious doctrines, for the overwhelming majority of religious denominations taught creeds in which a personal relationship between each individual and his God was established, without interposition of ecclesiastical officials or orders promulgated by human beings.

This did not solve, however, the problem which was crucial after the Revolution had been won: the problem of protection of the people in their rights and privileges and the establishment of the sovereignty of the people. Government of some form was necessary, and a few years showed that national government was necessary. Even state governments were hard to swallow, but for some years the idea of a national government was too much to stomach. A loose confederation of independent states was formed with a constitution called Articles of Confederation, but it collapsed because it established no real government on a national scale. And during those years of trial, the United States came nearer to anarchy than ever in its history. John Fiske's name for it, "the critical period," has come into popular use; it seemed critical indeed.

Two features in the period of Thomas Jefferson's life have already been named as outstanding examples to support the views of those who interpret our history as a series of individual miracles performed by God for the benefit of the American people. One of the main facets of the second was the writing, signing and ratification of the Constitution. Hundreds, if not thousands, of students of the period have written extensively of the apparently miraculous nature of these procedures. Their dramatic quality needs no elaboration here.

Like the Declaration of Independence, the Constitution is really two documents, not one. In an earlier section I have said that the Constitution might well be called the Declaration of Self-Government, and this applies particularly to those portions which may be called the first of the two documents. Such a document, if the portions were rearranged and collected, would comprise the Preamble, which not only states the purposes of the Constitution, but announces that it is an instrument of the people, who are sovereign; the statement of the authority and power of the Constitution, from Article VI; and the provision for amending it at any time. These statements and provisions come nearer than perhaps any other document in history to forming an eternal code of government.

The second document, comprising the balance of the original Constitution and the Bill of Rights, is at the same time a further guarantee of the rights of the people and an outline of a unique form of parliamentary, representative government. This document has been altered in hundreds of ways since 1787, through the twenty-one amendments. These alterations have been of a major character, such as provisions for basic changes in the citizenship status of Americans; the manner of election of the President, Vice President and Senators; the qualifications for voters; and the extension of many clauses applying only to the national government to cover the state governments also.

If we were to revert to the Constitution of 1787, even with the Bill of Rights added, Americans would feel that we were far from democracy as we know it, and conservatives and liberals alike would protest vehemently. But what I have called the first document gave the Constitution the flexibility needed "to form a more perfect union." And that such an approach to democratic government emerged from the bewilderment and near-despair of the post-Revolution days is an indication of another victory in the many seemingly hopeless struggles which make up our history.

An entirely different phase of the writing of the Constitution must be understood in order to know the story of the American people during the life of Thomas Jefferson. So far we have dealt largely with the political developments of the colonies and of the new nation. European civilization, both as something to import and as something from which to escape, has been viewed in the light of Europe's political concepts of the time, expressed in the divine-right theory and its ramifications. Like all political concepts, these had an economic basis, and the economic basis of life in the colonies grew increasingly important as communities developed, farming became widely practiced, and manufacturing, industry and trade became established.

In the pre-United States world of North America, as has been described, two strong movements existed and flourished. One was the movement to build a colonial empire, using slaves for the purpose. The other was the movement to import European civilization, whose economic aspects I have deferred mentioning until now. Broadly, these two movements were counterparts of movements throughout the Western world, feudalism and capitalism. The latter was gradually, but in irregular steps, replacing the former, and the change was at its highest point of acceleration in England. Both of these movements moved bodily across the Atlantic to the New World.

Feudalism was represented both by the slaves and the semislaves, called indentured servants. Capitalism was represented by the so-called free men, who were released from personal restrictions on physical movement, change of occupation, opportunity to rise in the social and economic scale and who worked entirely on their own behalf and under their own mastership. Only in the colonies were these changes so marked as to be outwardly noticeable at first, for in Europe the change was much more gradual, and in fact has not been accomplished in many areas even today.

The basic differences between feudalism and capitalism lay in two fields. The first was that of the status and authority of the rulers, masters or (to use a modern term) bosses. The second was that of the status and relative freedom of subjects, servants or workers. Capitalism eliminated the divine-right status of masters, but in its earliest and unrestricted form, did not eliminate the masters. Instead, authority was transferred from those thought to be divinely appointed to rule to those who possessed economic power in the form of income-producing property, but who acted independently of one another.

Capitalism also changed the status of former serfs to that of free citizens, removing physical and social restrictions on their activities, and affording them opportunity to join the ranks of the masters when they acquired sufficient income-producing property. This change, more marked in the United States than anywhere else in the world, but also taking place slowly everywhere to some degree, was one of the epochal steps of world history.

The struggle between the two systems produced a new economic and social figure, who can best be described as the Common Man. Unlike the peasant or serf of former times, he was free to choose his occupation, to live a life according to the dictates of his own conscience and desires.

No longer could divinely appointed authorities compel him to serve them on grounds of law or divine authority.

On the other hand, the Common Man was unlike the new type of master, for he possessed no income-producing property and his subsistence depended on his own labor, the fruits of which he had to divide with the masters on a basis which, realistically considered, was not far from the old basis of feudalism. Economic power by the masters had replaced divinely authorized power by former masters, but the power still existed, though it was exercised differently. During this period, Adam Smith, the Scottish economist, wrote his powerful work, *The Wealth of Nations*, which is the classical account of the shift from feudalism to capitalism.

The Common Man did not spring into being overnight, but was a gradual development over a century and a half. By the time the Constitution was written, he had become a distinct but largely unrecognized entity; and the common people were and have been ever since the largest population group in the nation, with well over a majority of Americans in its ranks. The second population group was that of slaves and semislaves.

Two other population groups existing at that time were the colonial empire builders, those who owned the plantations, slaves and commercial establishments that made up the empire; and the income-producing property owners—agrarian, industrial, commercial and financial—who employed not slaves but the common people in their establishments. But what these two population groups lacked in numbers, they made up for in economic power and in influence derived from world-old concepts of aristocracy and master-servant relationships, which survived even when the divine-right theory had itself been pulverized.

Obviously there was a clash of interests among the four population groups. Fundamentally, there were two clashes, and unless both of them are recognized in their distinct aspects, most of American history is a baffling mystery. One was the clash between the two tiny groups, the empire builders or masters under a feudal system, and the income-producing property owners under the rising capitalist system.

For a variety of reasons too numerous to list, reasons which the reader undoubtedly knows as well as I, the interests of the latter group were best served by a strong national government; and the interests of the first group, which was constantly under attack and was already on the defensive, were for measures which would leave them undisturbed. These measures in the political sphere provided for the maintenance of sovereignty in the states where their empires lay and which they dominated.

In concrete terms, the scene was set for the conflict between a strong national government and what came to be called States' rights, and its first dramatic act was in the Constitutional Convention in Philadelphia in the summer of 1787.

The second fundamental clash of interests was equally potent in causing the conflict over States' rights, but for different reasons. This clash has been labeled by Macaulay and many other eminent historians before and since with a phrase that is a deceptive oversimplification: the poor

[62]

versus the rich. As the eighteenth century came to its final decade in the United States, the clash was between the common man, allied (though not yet conscious of it) with the slaves and semislaves; and the two tiny groups with economic power.

The common people, as has been said above, looked on all government as fettering the individual. Their political leaders, of whom Jefferson was the first in importance, even though he was not present at the writing of the Constitution because of his ambassadorship to France, were of the same mind, but realized that there must be some government; and they fought not only for recognition of the sovereignty of the people as a whole, but also for protection of individual rights.

They and the people differed on the issue of Federal power versus States' Rights, largely because the industrialization of the North was just beginning, and in the agrarian economy of the northern states, the common man did not to any great extent feel any clash between himself and the owners of income-producing property; living on his farm, or working on another's farm, his concern was with local government, not state or national. But on the whole, protection of States' rights seemed closer to preservation of individual liberty than the establishment of a national government, reminiscent of the hated British rule of former days. Most of the people's leaders, like Jefferson, took this view.

So one of the most astonishing alliances in all history took place, an alliance between the leaders of the common people and the tiny group of colonial empire builders. As the years passed, the two groups and their thinking became inextricably interwound, as the Civil War half a century or more later was to show.

After satisfactory compromises had been worked out, and the Constitution had been written, ratified and reinforced with the Bill of Rights, the clash between the common people and the propertied interests began to reveal itself. The Constitution, in its authors' effort to find a substitute for divinely appointed rulers, had firmly established a basis of sovereignty in the people, but by tradition had provided for positions of power in the governmental structure to be assigned to members or representatives of the economically powerful groups.

The President was an example. A system in which political parties would exist, representing different groups or different principles, was not envisioned, and the provisions for the President's election were that the two candidates receiving the highest number of electoral votes would become respectively President and Vice President.

As for Congress, the Senate, which in addition to legislative power was given powers in connection with appointments to executive and judicial offices and in the approval of treaties, was not to be elective at all. That body was thought of as being made up of a group of what are now popularly called "elder statesmen," though physically they need not be old, appointed by the state legislatures, presumably agreeing on all fundamental issues and amicably working out relatively minor differences of opinion.

Only the House of Representatives was to be elected directly by the people, and if it passed unwise laws, the

[64]

Senate could easily remedy the matter by not acting on them.

During the first three Presidential terms, those of Washington and that of John Adams, the clash of interests became public, political parties were organized, and the roseate dream of the Constitution makers ended. It fell to the lot of Thomas Jefferson to become the first President championing the Common Man.

After Jefferson's first election, the Constitution was amended, in 1804, changing the provisions for Presidential elections, so that political parties could function as they do now. The Twelfth Amendment provides that separate ballots be cast for President and Vice President, eliminating the original idea that the second highest Presidential candidate should become Vice President. This made party tickets possible.

All these developments, however, were simply shadows cast in advance of the impending clashes and struggles of the next period of our history. Two years after Jefferson died came the first great climax in these clashes, with the election of Andrew Jackson, and an entirely new era began.

The world of Thomas Jefferson was crowded with mighty events, but greater than any of the specific events in this eighty-three year period were the main streams of progress, which can be summarized as the establishment of religious liberty, self-government, state and national independence; the overthrow of foreign ties; tremendous geographical expansion and settling of new communities, states and territories; and long strides toward universal public education.

[65]

Even more vividly than in the colonial period of North America, this period demonstrated that the struggles of religious men and women were animated by more than economic pressures or the inclinations of "human nature." The souls of men were on the march under God, with growing understanding of the possibilities and richness of life. An unusually penetrating analysis of developments of this character was made in 1946 by William Benton, then Assistant Secretary of State and now United States Senator from Connecticut, in an address about the American missionary movement. Referring to the history of the immortal saying of Jesus, "Ye shall know the truth, and the truth shall make you free," he said:

You will recall that when Jesus uttered this sentence, He explained that by *truth* He meant the fact of His divinity and power of salvation, and that by *free* He meant freedom from sin. . . . But during the ages since Jesus spoke the words, they have acquired a new and additional meaning. . . . In this new meaning, *truth* signifies knowledge—knowledge of the world and of the people in it; of the actions and opinions of men, wise and foolish; of the arts and sciences of medicine, agriculture, engineering, economics, and so on; of the ways in which human beings live together in communities and nations, and their hopes and dreams and fears and needs.

And in this new meaning, *free* refers to the liberation of men from tyranny, political shackles, social suppressions, economic slavery, and all institutions that limit their beliefs, dim their aspirations, or curb their love for their fellow human beings.

4. THE WORLD OF ABRAHAM LINCOLN
1809-1865

THE MOST DISTINGUISHED FIGURE ever to have lived in the State of Indiana was, on the Fourth of July, 1826, a tall, gangling, seventeen-year-old farm laborer.

He was as representative of the earlier type of common people in the United States, in many respects, as might have been found by modern surveys and prize contests. His family name was derived from a county of England, Lincolnshire. His first name had been selected, as was then customary in many parts of the United States, from among the names of Old Testament heroes, none of whom was greater than Abraham.

Like many other Americans, he had been born in poverty and had grown up in the humblest possible way, keeping alive by grim battles against the forces of the wilderness. Like other Americans, he had the advantages of free movement, choice of occupation and the opportunity—even though difficult to take advantage of—to acquire education and learning. Born in Kentucky, he had with his family made his way over mountains and rivers to the newly created state of Indiana, and was soon to make adventurous journeys all the way to New Orleans, and later to settle in

[67]

another distant area, Illinois. Trained for a meager life of farm labor, he was to become a capable lawyer, a Congressman and an immortal President.

The biographies of Lincoln I have seen do not record his reaction when the news made its way to the wooded lanes and sparsely inhabited fields of Spencer County, Indiana, that John Adams and Thomas Jefferson, the second and third presidents of the United States, had died on the same day—the nation's fiftieth anniversary of the signing of the Declaration of Independence. He probably considered the incident, as did most of his neighbors, an interesting coincidence. It really was more than this, for it symbolized the end of an era in United States history and the birth of an entirely new one. The day was to come when Abraham Lincoln himself would become a symbol, a symbol of all that is great in democracy and religion, but that day was a third of a century in the future, and it was well that he was unwittingly preparing himself for his unforgettable role by the simple process of being one of the common people.

We have seen that Thomas Jefferson left behind him a nation of about eleven million people and twenty-four states. In the brief span between Lincoln's birth in 1809 and Jefferson's death in 1826, about four million of these had been born or had migrated to the United States, and seven of the twenty-four states had joined the Union. But this was only a beginning, for as the youth grew to manhood and went on to his eventual end, he saw the population more than triple, rising to about thirty-five million in 1865; and during the same period the number of states rose to thirty-six. The nation swept unbrokenly from the

Atlantic to the Pacific, with nearly the same vast area that it possesses today.

It was emphatically an era of the common people, who were multiplying and moving and developing a people's civilization, irrepressible, overflowing with energy, overthrowing traditions, demanding rights and exercising them. It was the era when the word "democracy" came into common use—a word neither the Declaration of Independence nor the Constitution had employed—and when the essential principles of these documents were forged into human experience and law and practice. It was an era when religion, not as an instrument of piety or repression, but as a surge of warmth and brotherhood and love flowed through men's veins like fire and made them shout within their hearts, "I *am* my brother's keeper." "We *will* do unto others as we would have others do unto us." "We *will* know the truth and the truth *shall* make us free."

But it is not to be expected that this was the whole story of that era. Like every other period of our history, this was one of struggle, nearly always struggle against forces that seemed mightier than could ever be conquered. There were many defeats, many collapses, many tragedies, many postponements, many advances by the enemies of progress and by self-seekers.

I shall not attempt even to mention all the stirring events of the world of Abraham Lincoln, for not only is it outside the province of this work, but many historians have covered the period painstakingly and brilliantly, vividly and profoundly. The elections and deeds of Andrew Jackson, of whom it may be said (as it has been said about a great modern author in relation to an earlier one) that he was not greater than Thomas Jefferson but stood on his shoulders; the long and complicated struggle over the Bank of the United States and the establishment of the United States Treasury; the ups and downs of our tariff policy; the annexation of Texas and the wresting of California from Mexico; the holocaust that is called the Civil War, or if you prefer, the War between the States—these and many more happenings were as important in our total history as any that preceded or followed them. But, as in former sections, I simply want to point out some of the principal factors in this period that shaped the movements toward democracy and that demonstrate how this nation has developed under God.

To each period of our history there seem to be attached one or more popularly believed but largely mythical stories or interpretations of events. We have had occasion already to explore briefly the story relating to the bounteous New World simply waiting to be visited by Europeans to disgorge its wealth; and also the inaccurate interpretation of the structure of the United States government as being almost a duplicate of those of Rome and Athens. Two more such accounts have been widely disseminated, and sometimes taught in our schools, with little more foundation in fact than the earlier ones.

One of these mythical stories is that the ratification of the Constitution and the Bill of Rights automatically made the United States a republic, and that their provisions applied to the whole nation in every respect. Thus, many people are under the impression that the First Amendment established freedom of religion and of speech throughout the country, or at least guaranteed it; that "cruel and unusual punishment" for crime was barred everywhere; and so on down a list of scores of Constitutional provisions. Few of us have not heard orators at patriotic assemblages and radio speakers voice such opinions. Yet the facts are entirely different.

It is true that the Constitution proclaimed the sovereignty of the people and outlined the principle that all law and all government were subject to the will of the people. But as a working document, the Constitution created a national government of extremely limited powers, and in the main its original regulations, statements of rights and privileges, prohibitions and restrictions applied not to the people nor to the state governments, which were sovereign in many fields, but to Congress and the national government alone.

Congress, for example, was forbidden to interfere by law with free speech or a free press, but the states were not. Federal courts were barred from meting out cruel and unusual punishments, but state and county and local courts were not. Congress and the officers of the national government were to be elected or appointed by representatives of the people, but had no power to define the qualifications for voters or to assure any person the right to vote at all. Large areas of human activity, such as education, marriage and divorce, bankruptcy procedures, corporation charters, land ownership, care of the destitute, aged, helpless, insane, were almost entirely out of the purview of the national government and Congress.

Obviously, then, both the Declaration of Independence

[71]

and the Constitution were magnificent statements of the principles and ideals of democracy, and the latter, considering the age in which it was written, was a remarkable pattern for representative government, which could be adapted to the needs of state governments and to the desires of the people. But the work of democratizing the states and assuring the people everywhere of their "unalienable rights" was only beginning. The years of the era of Thomas Jefferson, and later the era of Abraham Lincoln, particularly the latter, were filled with the struggles involved in this process. These struggles were countless and were waged on every kind of front.

In the field of political life, most states had both religious and property qualifications for voting. In some, the right to vote was restricted to Christians, in others to Protestants alone. Property qualifications were usually high. There were property qualifications for state officeholders too; in one or two instances an official had to be almost the equivalent of a millionaire to qualify for high office. In other fields, imprisonment for debt was one of the most grievous customs, and it was almost universal. Capital punishment was the penalty for many crimes, some of them now called misdemeanors. Torture and beatings and disfigurement were common penalties for crime.

One by one, over the years, within each state the struggles were waged desperately, determinedly, slowly, against the resistance of the politically and economically powerful. As always, they were waged by the people themselves, who eventually found leaders to espouse their causes. And one by one, the barriers were lowered, the processes of democracy were extended. When in 1829 Andrew Jackson was elected President, most of the propertied and "respectable" shuddered, for he symbolized the rise of the Common Man, and his opponents felt the end of the nation was at hand, with anarchy about to reign supreme.

It seems to me that no one can live through this period in his mind and heart, read the accounts of the day-by-day lives of the American people through the first half of the nineteenth century, watch the ragged, irregular front lines in the vanguard of the people ever moving forward despite all obstacles, without a deep realization of the presence of God and His inspiration. I think the greatest arrogance in human history lies in the assumption over the centuries by some groups that God is, despite all biblical statements to the contrary, on the side of the economically powerful few, and blesses them in their efforts to keep the people of the world under their subjugation.

I have said before, as I shall say again, that in the spectacle of a whole people moving forward under impulses so profound that it hardly recognizes them, so strong that it denies the evidence of eyes and ears, so selfless that individual identities are almost lost, lies the most comprehensive tribute to God and His goodness and power that our history offers.

It is perhaps appropriate here to quote a sentence or two from a sermon delivered on February 26, 1860, by Henry Ward Beecher, which Abraham Lincoln heard:

Now nothing can be more untrue than that God works completed things. I do not know but there are instances to be found in which God wills, and the thing stands instantly up according to his will; but I will say this: that the law of Divine working, so far as we are able to ascertain it, is the reverse of this. In human life, and in the natural world, perfection is evolved through stages of self-growth. This is so throughout the whole realm of life. . . . God works in you, but not for you. He never does your work. He works in you not only to will, but to do.

There was a second erroneous interpretation of events that flourished in the world of Abraham Lincoln. This interpretation has flourished ever since to some extent. This had as its basis the idea that something called the American System was a unique economic system born and nurtured in the English colonies, and brought to maturity as the United States became a nation. According to this theory, the Declaration of Independence was signed, the Revolution was fought, and the Constitution was written and ratified for the sole purpose of establishing what is commonly known as Western capitalism. I have spared no effort to portray our nation as unique in its beginnings as well as in its development; but if there was one feature of it that was not unique, it was the economic system which developed to replace feudalism.

Its theories of the sacred nature of property rights; of an aristocracy based on wealth instead of on divinely given powers; of competition as the automatic regulator of prices, high quality of products and freedom of opportunity; of desire for great financial reward as a dominant motive in the conduct of most people; of individual risk as the price of financial freedom, were all borrowed or imported bodily from Great Britain and Europe, where capitalism spread through every area that saw the collapse of feudalism.

[74]

To call this the American System has no more basis in fact than to call it the Norwegian System or the Bulgarian System or the Italian System or the British System. For more than a century it has been the standard economic system of the whole world, barring those areas in which feudalism has persisted, and latterly, those in which other economic systems have arisen.

In order to avoid all misunderstanding, I must say at this point that I am a firm adherent and strong supporter of the private-enterprise system as it has developed and has been modified by the people of the United States—and later sections of this sketch will try to describe briefly those developments and modifications. I think that our economic system is the best the world has yet found to promote the material and spiritual interests of mankind, and to preserve the liberties and sovereignty of the people.

But to assert that the capitalism of our early days was the unique achievement of the Founding Fathers is not only to be inaccurate, but to miss the whole point of the greatness of our nation. It was not a unique economic system which our forefathers established. Our political system was unique, but even here the basic greatness of our nation was not fully revealed. In the eternal accounting the length of the President's term of office, or the fact of having two legislative bodies instead of one, or the precise manner in which Supreme Court justices are appointed will not amount to very much. Our greatness lies in the spiritual basis which was established for human relations: the world-shaking belief in human equality and brotherhood.

And in no period did this spiritual basis and movement

[75]

display itself more clearly than during Abraham Lincoln's life, cutting through economic considerations, riding rough-shod over profit-and-loss accounts, risking the nation's life itself for principles that were greater than the nation, greater than the whole material world.

In the preceding section we noted the industrial develop-ment of the nation and its bringing to the fore a clash between the Common Man and the owners of income-producing property. It was as this clash became more vivid and was climaxed during the eight years of Andrew Jackson's administration and during the following four of Martin Van Buren's, that the nation began to see that the clash had become implicit and inevitable when the Declara-tion of Independence was signed and when the United States government was established under the Constitution, even though the Founding Fathers had been unaware of it.

With industrial development and expansion came enor-mous growth in individual financial, commercial and indus-trial enterprises; multiplying payrolls; and great diminution in the number of self-owned, self-managed, self-operated concerns. By leaps and bounds the common people were plunged into work for impersonal masters, in both agricul-ture and industry. As they gained political rights and privileges, they found themselves losing economic rights and privileges, consisting of the rights to determine their own destinies and to make even a bare living when times were bad.

Abraham Lincoln had hardly reached manhood when the first of those periodical economic cataclysms which have featured almost every decade ever since, occurred. They were variously called panics, depressions, recessions, hard times. During them, some of the wealthy were hurled from their positions of power and affluence; the savings and property of smaller figures of respectability were swept away; and the common people, strong, able, anxious to work, became to a great extent destitute and helpless. It was reminiscent of the fifteenth and sixteenth centuries in Europe, when unemployment became a strong motivating force for the settlement of the New World.

The reactions to these developments were varied. To the common people, the time seemed to have come to revert to the principles enunciated by Thomas Jefferson in the Declaration of Independence, and to put them into practice. To the propertied interests, the time seemed to have come to reconsider all the foolishness of the revolutionary days and all the heresies expressed by the Declaration of Independence.

True, they felt that King George III had been an old fool and we were well rid of him and all the notions about the divine right of kings and their appointed subordinates. But the basic principle of a ruling class was sound and valid, for the common people could not be trusted. It was thought symbolic that the foolish king had been replaced by one of the wealthiest men in the United States, George Washington. An aristocracy based on wealth was the obvious thing that God desired; it came to be called "a natural aristocracy," and its defense along democratic lines was that anyone could join that aristocracy, regardless of his birth or descent, by the easy process of becoming wealthy.

So a strange doctrine began to be widely preached during

the 1820's and 1830's, strange in the land in which the embattled farmers "fired the shot heard 'round the world" a half century before. I am sorry to report that many apostles of religion were enlisted in the promulgation of that doctrine. American churches, assembly halls and outdoor meeting places resounded, as did many American newspapers and the halls of Congress, with fervid espousals and explanations of the inequality of man. God Himself was vouched for as the Author of this state of affairs, and His will and His plan should not be disputed. Even today, not-so-faint echoes of this doctrine can be heard from time to time.

Perhaps the best summary of this doctrine is contained in a letter purported to have been written by Lord Macaulay to the American historian, Randall, many years later, in 1857. Only a part of it is quoted in order to give the gist of his thought:

I have long been convinced that institutions purely democratic must, sooner or later, destroy liberty or civilization, or both. . . . I have not the smallest doubt that, if we had a purely democratic government here, the effect would be the same. Either the poor would plunder the rich and civilization would perish, or order and prosperity would be saved by a strong military government, and liberty would perish. . . . In bad years there is plenty of grumbling here, and sometimes a little rioting. But it matters little, for here the sufferers are not the rulers. The supreme power is in the hands of a class, numerous indeed, but select; of an educated class; of a class which is, and knows itself to be, deeply interested in the security of property and maintenance of order. Accordingly, the malcontents are firmly yet gently restrained. The bad time is got over without robbing the wealthy to relieve the indigent. . . .

It is quite plain that your government will never be able to restrain a distressed and discontented majority in the government, which has the rich, who are always a minority, absolutely at its mercy. . . . Which of . . . two candidates is likely to be preferred by a workingman who hears his children cry for more bread? . . . There will be, I fear, spoliation. The spoliation will increase the distress. The distress will produce fresh spoliation. There is nothing to stop you. Your Constitution is all sail and no anchor. . . . Thinking thus, of course, I cannot reckon Jefferson among the benefactors of mankind. . . .

To repeat, the common people were not entirely happy about the promulgation of a doctrine like this. And they made their influence felt, as the years passed, until its promulgators reached a momentous decision in American history, one little recognized until one of our great modern historians pointed it out. He is Arthur M. Schlesinger, Jr., whose *Age of Jackson* not only won a Pulitzer Prize, but has also been hailed, in the words of a noted critic, as "a landmark in historical literature." Mr. Schlesinger sets at about 1840 the time when the promulgators of the antidemocracy, antiequality doctrine decided that they were barking up the wrong tree. Up to this time they had to be given the same credit for honesty of purpose and frankness of expression which characterized the Holy Alliance of 1815; Metternich's expressions, previously quoted in these pages; and Lord Macaulay's later ideas, quoted above. But they realized it was a losing struggle, and so they changed—not their beliefs at all, but their expressions—and became public advocates of democracy, and have been ever since. In Schlesinger's phrase, "conservatism was streamlined for the Jacksonian world," and ever since that time our grandfathers, our fathers and we ourselves have had to judge all political candidates by reading between the lines. No longer are there candidates for political office espousing anti-democracy in public. They are all for democracy and the rule of the people in their general pronouncements. Only by their specific actions can we decide on what side they are.

The importance of this change was so great that its effect ever since on the life of the American people is hard to estimate. The difficulties of choosing political candidates and causes on the basis of public statements were only part of the trouble. The same change also marked the rise of a curious, two-front attitude among individuals which exists even today. This is a sort of personal separation between Church and State inside one's soul, where Church and State should never be separated. It brought a stifling of religious impulses if they affected the operation of a set of cold and callous principles which guided active conduct.

Thus a man, devoutly and sincerely, could believe that he was his brother's keeper, and proclaim this belief to the world in church and in pious private conversations. At the same time he could be indifferent to the welfare of those about him and blandly carry out in his business such principles as, "The devil take the hindmost," "Each man for himself" and "Your troubles are no problem of mine." He could endorse heartily the actions of the good Samaritan and at the same time witness with indifference destitution, suffering and helplessness on the part of his neighbors.

In effect, two personal codes of conduct were set up, one

for Sunday use and the other for practical operations, which clashed with each other. There was nothing new about this, in a sense, for hypocrisy is as old as religion itself; but this was not plain hypocrisy. People came actually to be unconscious of the contradictions in their lives, and to think, when considering either of the two codes, that it was fine and patriotic and according to the dictates of God.

In this period, perhaps more than in any other, the curious two-front personal attitude came to be embodied in our language, by alterations of the original meanings of words and the coining of new words and phrases. By this device, people were enabled to express open contempt for principles which in one inner compartment they approved; and conversely, to extol others which in another inner compartment they condemned. The same man might be praised at one time for having "vision" and at another time be derided as a "dreamer," because the word "vision" came to mean nothing more than an earthy comprehension of material possibilities. "Practical" was emptied of all content of the spiritual life, and was used as a supreme compliment. "Success" began to refer only to money-getting prowess. Those who were humane and gentle were denounced as being "soft." In current days, we know that persons with a passion for justice and mercy are publicly ridiculed as "do-gooders" and "bleeding hearts." An "idealist" is automatically dubbed a "crackpot." Men boast of being "hard-headed," whatever that means, and "down-to-earth." Selfishness and greed have become virtues, in the guise of "enlightened self-interest," a term that would have perhaps puzzled Jesus. Along with these words and phrases, others which express equally strong convictions about religion and nobility in life have been and are in constant use.

The change also marked, because of the similarity of public expressions, a great lessening of the actual differences among political parties which bore varying labels. As the years passed beyond the period of Abraham Lincoln, there were scores of occasions when the two dominant political parties, the Republican and the Democratic, were literally so much alike that only their labels and the names of their candidates differentiated them. Even their political platforms became almost interchangeable.

But even with this "streamlining" technique the campaigns advocating return to an old order continued and grew through and beyond the period of Lincoln. Conditions favored the growth of giant fortunes, monopoly, speculation, financial crimes, extortion, crashes, waves of unemployment.

Despite these untoward developments, this period was fundamentally one of tremendous growth among the people. The acquiring of political rights was steady and unceasing. Although great poverty existed, the percentage of those living in relative comfort steadily increased. Public education spread by leaps and bounds. The observance of law and order and the improvement of judicial and penal procedures were marked in ever larger areas of the nation. Per capita income increased. Transportation and communications both took mighty strides. Just as the democratizing within states carried the principles of the Constitution into the lives of more and more people, so among the states and their inhabitants a feeling of national solidarity and unity grew.

While all these developments were taking place, another movement that cut across, through, beneath and above them all was sweeping the nation. This was the movement to end physical human slavery, and to bring to disintegration the whole colonial empire system which had existed for two hundred years. There has never been another movement like this one against slavery. It was largely leaderless, and only a handful of those who led it are known even by name today. It was opposed or ignored by virtually all prominent leaders of the time. It was in opposition to nearly all economic interests and considerations. It was unaided by the slaves themselves. It was motivated solely by religious impulses among the people and by the determination that, whatever else happened, all men should possess physical freedom.

The antislavery movement represented the greatest single demonstration of religious fervor, not only in the life of the United States, but in all human history, and it symbolized as nothing else ever has the power of God in aiding the weak in a colossal struggle against what seemed every conceivable physical concentration of power that existed.

The Crusades of the Middle ages, with their plumed and panoplied aristocrats accompanied by their slaves, semislaves and mercenaries, bent on torturing, enslaving and killing hundreds of thousands of people in the name of the Prince of Peace, pale beside this moving spectacle of a whole people rising against the greatest of crimes— human slavery.

It has been said that the Civil War represented a struggle of the strong against the weak, for the Union forces in power were many times greater than those of the South;

and also that underlying the issue of slavery, and even of so-called States' rights, were the economic interests and desires of the powerful capitalists of the North. There is much truth in these claims, but the Civil War was only the climax of the struggle against slavery, and only during its four years were the opponents of slavery the physically stronger side. In all the preceding years, which made the war and the freeing of the slaves inevitable, it was pre-eminently another of the struggles of the weak against the strong which have characterized the history of the United States.

The Civil War brought to Abraham Lincoln the opportunity to fill a role which has influenced the whole world ever since. He was a curious President, unique in his differences from those who preceded and those who followed him. Unlike others, in his path to the Presidency he had exerted virtually no influence on his time. Until his first election he was unaccomplished and virtually unknown, except as a poor boy who had become a fairly able lawyer and at one time had served a term in Congress as a Representative. He had taken no stand against slavery, although he had opposed its further extension into new territories.

Indeed, in his First Inaugural Address in 1861 he declared: "I have no purpose, directly or indirectly, to interfere with the institution of slavery in the States where it exists. I believe I have no lawful right to do so, and I have no inclination to do so." Nor had Lincoln taken any marked stand on any of the other issues of the day relating to the rise of monopoly and the rights of the people.

As President, Lincoln's military direction of the war was

by no means outstanding, and military historians agree that the performance of the South was far more brilliant. The signing of the Emancipation Proclamation came only after two years of continuous urging by Lincoln's advisers. And historians tell us that the forces of monopoly and opposition to fundamental democracy grew immensely in strength and power during the whole war.

Yet Lincoln was one of the most important and valuable figures in our history, whose influence has done more than perhaps that of any other single man to inspire the people of the United States in their building of a great nation under God. This was because, as I see it, his overwhelming desire to preserve the Union, combined with the richness of his human sympathy for his fellow men, the breadth of his democratic vision and the simple eloquence of his words, lifted him to a position as spokesman for the roots of democracy and apostle of the aspirations of our people for freedom.

He stands as a unique character in our history, set apart from its detailed struggles and economic and social day-by-day developments, symbolizing the basic greatness of human equality and brotherhood. Three of his documents alone—his letter to Mrs. Bixby, the Gettysburg Address and the Second Inaugural Address—were enough to bring him immortality. His pleas to follow the paths of God, his stern denunciation of our vanity and self-righteousness in turning from God (illustrated by the quotation from him on page 145), his injunctions to fill our lives and actions with the Lord's teachings, remain his great gift to humanity.

5. THE WORLD OF WOODROW WILSON
1856-1924

THE READER WILL FIND that the remainder of this historical
sketch is briefer than the preceding sections. It is not
because the manifestations of God and His power and goodness have been less frequent in the latter years of our national life.

But we have now surveyed briefly the rise and development of the United States from the colonial landings at
Jamestown, Virginia, to the assassination of Abraham Lincoln, a period of 258 years. Eighty years remain to bring us
to the chronological limit which I have set for this sketch,
the death of Franklin Roosevelt in 1945. In point of time,
the later period makes up less than a quarter of our national
history. I think this is a wholesome realization, particularly
if you agree with me that the first or second decade of a
man's life is ordinarily as important—perhaps more important—in determining his total character, as any given later
decade.

At any given time, this long perspective is hard to
achieve. Woodrow Wilson, whose world we are now considering, once said, "America does not march, as so many
other peoples march, looking back over its shoulder." But

Woodrow Wilson the historian would have been the first to agree that the forward look at any moment is the result of other forward looks in past moments, years and centuries.

There is a tendency today to think of the past half century or quarter century or whole century as the entire history of the United States, and to feel that people here and elsewhere were never before faced with the crucial problems of today, that in some mysterious way the world was created, not six thousand or sixty thousand or six million years ago, but in 1848 or 1896 or 1917 or 1945. One of the most valuable statistical and historical surveys of recent years, crammed with amazing data about our people, seems to be based on the assumption that the United States was plumped down on the North American continent, with more than thirty million souls and a continent-wide physical expanse, all neatly created in the wink of an eye and in full operation.

Another reason for the relative brevity of these sections telling of the worlds of Woodrow Wilson and Franklin Roosevelt is that as each of us approaches the days of his own lifetime, his interpretations of events tend to be personal opinions rather than interpretations based on acknowledged facts. When I was born, Woodrow Wilson was only twenty-six, and Franklin Roosevelt was slightly less than seventeen months old. I was with Wilson two days before his physical collapse in 1919, and I not only worked with Franklin Roosevelt in his campaign for the Vice Presidency in 1920, but was a friend and adviser of his during his entire Presidential career. So the worlds of these two belong in large part to the world that is mine. While these facts will not diminish the vigor of my interpretations, I refrain from trying to decipher or explain God's immediate purposes in the years recently passed. I am fully conscious that others as religious, as well-informed and as sincere as I may differ widely with many of my interpretations.

If this work helps to make the reader proud of being an American, conscious of the goodness and power of God in our destiny, aware of the growth and strength of our desire for human brotherhood and the mutual sharing of responsibility, I shall be satisfied.

A final reason for not elaborating on the events of the years between 1865 and 1945 is twofold. More has been written about these years and their events than about any other period in the history of the world; and in the scope of this study of our people under God, there are just four developments of a fundamental nature that require discussion. One is our enormous increase in individual productivity. The second is the movement to protect our people from the depredations of unrestricted individual rapacity, monopoly and plutocracy. The third is the rise of a new concept of government as not merely a restrictive and regulatory force, but as an instrument of the people to assure education, opportunity, employment and security among themselves. And the fourth is a new concept of world unity and brotherhood. In their broad outlines, these can be presented with relative brevity.

Let us now glance at the world of Woodrow Wilson. He was nine years old when Lincoln died. His childhood and youth were filled with memories and tales of the Civil War and with experiences of its aftermath. During these years and for many years thereafter, these remained the chief subjects of political discussion among the American people. But despite the common absorption in these subjects and their manifold problems, bigger issues were at stake.

By 1865, the United States had emerged from its position as a small, new, revolutionary, heterogeneous country and had become one of the mightiest powers on earth. Its people had a standard of living comparable to, and in most cases far superior to, that of any other nation in the world, and a degree of independence far beyond that of other peoples. In military and naval power, the recently concluded war had demonstrated that it ranked as high as any national state on the globe.

When Lincoln died, the population was thirty-five million, a tremendous figure in comparison to European countries. The United States had a larger population than Great Britain or any European country except France and Russia (which was partly in Asia). Its inhabitants were more numerous than those of Greece, Denmark, Switzerland, the Netherlands, Portugal, Belgium, Sweden and Norway, all put together. It had more than twice as many people as Spain, nearly twice as many as Italy, millions more than Great Britain, Austria, or what is now Germany, only slightly fewer than France. In area, all of Europe and Great Britain (except Russia), covered only 45 per cent of the square miles that made up the vast expanse of the United States.

Moreover, our country had become truly continental, for the thirteen original states, with Vermont and Maine, contained less than half the nation's inhabitants. Unnumbered

[89]

highways and post roads, scores of thousands of miles of railroad track, four thousand miles of telegraph lines, thousands of newspapers and other periodicals were in existence.

At this time, while the slave and plantation owners of the South had been bankrupted, the propertied interests both in the South and in the North were for practical purposes supreme. Over the years, their power increased and the national government became almost openly subservient to them. Immigration leaped in a startling way, reaching the rate of more than a million a year, providing an immense labor pool which was an effective barrier to the rise of the labor movement.

Trusts were formed, gigantic consolidations of financial and industrial enterprises. So wealthy did some individuals become, and so widespread were large corporate interests that a new adaptation of the old "natural aristocracy" theory was devised to salve the consciences of the wealthy in the presence of hordes of destitute and unemployed people, and to explain to the poor on religious or pious lines that all was as it should be. This adaptation was the "stewardship" concept, in which certain individuals had been chosen by the grace of God not to own vast fortunes in reality, but merely to act as stewards holding the fortunes in trust for the ultimate benefit of mankind. Public piety, immense charitable donations for education, research, physical relief, became an unwritten law to guide those with swollen fortunes.

The people pursued in this same period two struggles: (1) the struggle for comforts; and (2) the struggle for survival. In addition, countless movements for individual and group rights and privileges were continued assiduously. Despite all obstacles, the people moved forward. They became more literate, more cultured, more mature. Because of great strides in individual productivity, wages and income inevitably increased, though not in proportion to the increases in profits. A growing sense of injustice spread over the land.

The last decade of the nineteenth century began bringing concrete results in the struggle of the people against the monopolies. A movement arose to use the national government to protect its citizens in concrete ways. The decade opened with the passage of the Sherman Antitrust Law, which was the first concrete evidence of the success of this movement, ineffective as it proved to be in practice. By 1896, a young and brilliant orator from Nebraska, William Jennings Bryan, arose to defy unrestricted and uncontrolled capitalism. The immediate issues of the campaign were trivial, but the basic issues were enormous, and Bryan nearly won the Presidential election.

The temper of the times was best illustrated when in 1899 the most sensational single event in the history of poetry occurred, the thunderous and world-wide response to the publication of "The Man with the Hoe," by a California school principal, Edwin Markham. While referring specifically to oppressed and subjugated peasants who were then plenteous in Europe, and while directing his denunciations concretely at "kingdoms and . . . kings," Markham's memorable blasts were addressed generally to "masters, lords and rulers in all lands," and were taken to apply to the workers of the United States as well as to other workers

[91]

throughout the world. He gave expression to thoughts shared by millions upon millions of his fellow countrymen when he wrote:

> There is no shape more terrible than this—
> More tongued with censure of the world's blind greed—
> More filled with signs and portents for the soul—
> More packed with danger to the universe.
>
> .   .   .   .
>
> Through this dread shape humanity betrayed,
> Plundered, profaned and disinherited,
> Cries protest to the Powers that made the world,
> A protest that is also prophecy.[1]

Although Bryan was narrowly defeated in 1896 and lost by increasing majorities in later campaigns, an accident brought to the fore Theodore Roosevelt, most of whose principles were opposed to those of Bryan, but who recognized many of the excesses of unrestricted capitalism. It was he who coined the phrase, "malefactors of great wealth." He caused to be enacted laws like the Pure Food and Drugs Act of 1906, and he used his executive power to curb owners of industry in times of strikes and industrial unrest. Even though his successor, William Howard Taft, did not follow precisely in his footsteps, the passage by Congress of the income tax amendment (which was perhaps the most important single piece of legislation ever to protect the people from the excesses of uncontrolled capitalism in all our history) occurred during his administration.

[1] *The Man with the Hoe and Other Poems* by Edwin Markham. Copyright 1899, by Doubleday and McClure Co., 1927, by Virgil Markham. Reprinted by permission.

The election of Woodrow Wilson showed the course upon which the people had decided. Even though his election was considered an accident due to the split in the Republican party, it was evidence of the trend of the people, for that split was caused by the rebellion of Theodore Roosevelt against some of the excesses of the moneyed interests and their refusal to sponsor him for the Presidency.

This period also was featured by another new movement, based on the concept of government as a co-operative endeavor for the provision of intangible and tangible needs of the people. While the Socialists, and the Communists later, were never able to work out a satisfactory method of introducing their economic systems without destroying many of the individual rights of the people, their aims and the soundness of much of their concept of government made a deep impression on the people of the United States. The influence of socialist or so-called socialist thinking began to be strong in local communities, states and the whole nation. Public ownership of utilities was discussed and widely adopted. Liberal city and state administrations were elected.

During the years of all these activities, an entirely different movement, now happily dead or in the throes of death, was arising. Fundamentally it was opposed to democratic concepts. This was the movement toward imperialism by the United States. Some of the aspects of the Spanish-American War and its aftermath symbolize this; in later years private exploitation of other countries, notably in Latin America, enforced by government military and financial forces, was indulged in with increasing vigor.

With the rise of balance-of-power clashes in Europe, still another movement arose, based on a new concept of world brotherhood. As we were led into World War I by the necessity of defending ourselves, Woodrow Wilson made the occasion one for envisioning and outlining new world relationships and activities.

With the end of the war, two things happened. The moneyed interests defeated the world co-operation plans and resumed almost complete control of the domestic economy; but also the backlog of all the exciting and constructive new movements and developments made the decade of 1920-30, one of the most constructive, sweeping and valuable in all our history.

Combined with this, there were reaction, irresponsibility, dishonesty in high places, almost total unawareness of what was happening to the nation, accompanied by the publicizing of a largely illusory condition symbolized by the phrase, "the jazz age." Books by Hemingway, Fitzgerald, Sinclair Lewis were considered representative of the conditions of the people, when actually they dealt with the problems and follies of only very small segments of the population. Newspapers and other periodicals ignored more and more the activities of the common people.

It was in the midst of this decade that Woodrow Wilson died, a broken man, apparently not realizing how God was at work, building the nation for a more glorious life than it had ever known. To see what that life has been like, we shall now look at the world of Franklin Roosevelt.

6. THE WORLD OF FRANKLIN ROOSEVELT

1882-1945

FRANKLIN ROOSEVELT WAS BEGINNING his forty-third year when Woodrow Wilson died. By no means a novice or youngster, he already bore the scars of political life, as a former member of the New York Legislature, as Assistant Secretary of the Navy, and as the unsuccessful candidate in 1920 for Vice President. He had witnessed the greater portion of the events in the development of the United States which Wilson had also witnessed, and which Wilson had helped to influence. The extent of Roosevelt's awareness, during that period, of the significance of those events will always be a mystery, no matter how many books and analyses of his life may be written in the future.

Certainly by birth, inheritance, family background and education, he seemed chiefly equipped to wave the banner of the moneyed interests. Why he did not do so, or why in later days he chose completely the cause of the common people, no one can say. The epithet which was frequently applied to him as President, in later years, "a traitor to his class," was an eloquent commentary on the deep cleavage that had existed from the latter days of Thomas Jefferson's Presidency, and that has existed up to the present time, with the espousal on the one hand of a "fair deal," and on the other, the denunciation of the dangers of "statism" or "the welfare state."

The theory has been advanced that the torturing physical disability which Roosevelt suffered in the 1920-30 decade did much to alter all his concepts of human values, and I shall be the last to deny the validity of this explanation.

More important than anything else, Roosevelt was a participant in the most significant decade in modern United States history, that of 1920-30, in the midst of which Woodrow Wilson died, as has been noted before. The clash of opposing forces in that decade was unprecedented, and its conflicts have accounted largely for almost everything that has happened since. In a preceding page I said of this decade, "The moneyed interests . . . resumed almost complete control of the domestic economy; but also the backlog of all the exciting new movements and developments made the decade of 1920-30 one of the most constructive, sweeping and valuable in all our history." The place has perhaps come to elaborate this statement.

One side of the picture was an enormous improvement in the conditions of the American people. Politically, there had been such laws as the woman's suffrage amendment to the Constitution, the Sherman and Clayton Acts and the income tax laws; there had been liberal movements nationally, in states, and in individual communities. The right to vote was constantly being extended. Education saw its greatest rise. Illiteracy reached new low records. High school education became standard among all groups. Colleges and universities expanded enormously. One-fourth of the total population attended educational institutions, as students or teachers. Leisure was greatly increased (average work hours decreased from seventy-two a week in 1850 to forty-seven in 1930). The average span of life had gone up from forty years to not far from fifty. The automobile and improved rail and water transportation had increased yearly per capita travel from five hundred to about twenty-four hundred miles. The radio had brought music, news, information and amusement cheaply into the home, and the movies provided inexpensive and often vivid outside entertainment. Electricity brought light to a large percentage of the people, power to farms and other domestic establishments. Sanitation, toilet facilities, plumbing and household appliances eased the working days of a large segment of the housekeepers of the nation. As in 1860, but on a far grander scale, the majority of the American people lived a more abundant life than the people of any other country in the world.

On the other side of the picture were a continuing rise in monopoly, concentration of economic power in a few hands, attempts to suppress civil and basic liberties and to regiment and standardize the lives, thoughts and beliefs of the American people in a fixed pattern of subservience to the misnamed "American System." Worst of all was the condition of destitution, permitted and ignored, among large segments of the people, a condition that Franklin Roosevelt was later to expose in his "Third-of-a-nation" speech.

So the gains alone did not satisfy the aspirations of the people. For a long time they had stopped being impressed by the fact that, on the whole, they were better off than other peoples (an argument which is still heard in defense of reactionary policies), for they had outgrown the feeling of belonging to an outpost of civilization that was more or less dependent on other and greater nations.

The American people considered that their ideals and struggles for liberty, abundance and equality made it inevitable that they should be not only better off than other peoples, but well off by their own standards. It was small comfort for a jobless, hungry worker or an impoverished farmer whom the sheriff had just dispossessed of his home and property to be told that he was a luckier person than a Hottentot or Englishman or Eskimo or Russian or Brazilian. And the decade that began with a great depression, continued with a form of restricted prosperity which included an unemployed group numbered in the millions by 1928.

This feeling of dissatisfaction was the direct result of the enormous increase in the productivity of workers, which I have named as the first of the four fundamental developments of this period. The increase in productivity, due to man's inventions and industrial machines, was simply the latest phase of man's ability to alter his environment; and just as this ability, as we have seen, played an all-important role in the original settling of the English colonies and the formation of the United States, so now it fundamentally altered the whole range of men's concepts of life, freedom and national conduct.

Once again we are brought to God's part in the building of our nation and our destiny, in giving to people who sought it and struggled for it against seemingly overwhelming odds, the strength and the opportunity to provide physical abundance—abundance not only for the nation as a whole, but abundance for each individual willing to be an active producer. The coming of an economy of abundance to replace an economy of scarcity was as revolutionary and overwhelming as the concepts of human equality and the people's sovereignty, which were envisioned and formulated by Thomas Jefferson and his associates.

For one thing, an entirely new orientation was given to former complaints and semirebellions, which were summed up by the expression attributed to Victor Hugo: "The rich will do everything for the poor except get off their backs." In an economy of scarcity, there is ground for debate regarding the proper distribution of the world's goods. A plausible case can be made, as in history it has been made, for the existence of a ruling class, a "natural aristocracy," based on wealth, to regulate things for the benefit of all. When there is not enough to go around, anyway, what the wealthy appropriate does not alter the poverty of the poor to any great extent. But in an economy of abundance, there is no discoverable reason why each individual should not share that abundance.

What seemed clearly wrong was the prevailing system of distribution, under which abundance, actual and potential, was not shared by the mass of the people, though it was there to share. Still worse, the system through periodical shake-ups of the economy, produced insecurity and want on every economic level. Nothing in this period of our history presented so many absurdities and resulted in so few attempts at rational explanation.

The feeling which arose among the people that the system needed alteration, and the actions that resulted from this feeling did not represent a mere resurgence of the movement that produced William Jennings Bryan and Edwin Markham's poem. This was more far-reaching. The second important development in this era, the movement to protect people from the depredations of unrestrained capitalism and economic rule by monopolies, was not the motivating force of this new feeling.

Actually, a totally new idea of government was born. Where before government had been seen as a regulatory and restrictive force, as well as a means of guaranteeing individual liberties, now it began to be seen also as a direct instrument of the people to perform educational, social and economic tasks for all. With this development, the religious concepts of human brotherhood and mutual co-operation were added to those of freedom and equality. The much-vaunted slogans, "Do-it-yourself," and "Do-it-alone," as guides to the abundant life were replaced, in the minds and hearts of millions of people, with the concept of "Let's do it together."

Proponents of the old order, however, were equally vigorous in their views. But I think that the proponents of the old order who are active today will largely agree that their leaders, both political and industrial, during the decade of 1920-30, if not later, were just about as unrealistic and irresponsible as King George III and his advisers were in an earlier era.

The first third of that decade was marked not only by a failure to cope with the postwar problems of war veterans and their families, and of inflation, which led inevitably to an economic crash in 1922, in which farmers and home owners lost their homes, and millions of willing workers were jobless. It was marked also by widespread corruption and graft participated in by high government officials and industrial magnates alike, which shocked the nation. During the rest of the decade, financial rectitude in government was restored, but a lack of awareness of the conditions of the common people existed to such a great extent as we find it almost impossible to believe, as we look back on it.

Also, the methods used to restore apparent prosperity, instead of being those of checking excesses, and adjusting profits, wages and prices in order to increase purchasing power, were to find foreign markets for so-called "excess" production (so-called not because the American people did not need the commodities produced, but because they could not afford to pay for them). The device used to enable foreign countries to purchase our "excess" production was to lend these countries the money to pay for what they bought, although the chance of their repaying the loans was remote.

Private steps to restore apparent prosperity were to make huge capital investments at inflated prices in plants and machinery, which were supposed to turn out the "excess" production for foreign countries; and for those with sufficient funds to indulge in an orgy of stock market and investment gambling which produced enormous paper profits, but had no effect on, or connection with, the common people, except to raise further the prices of their commodities.

Accordingly, the decade ended with the start of the greatest economic cataclysm in our history. It is hardly surprising that the national administration was hurled from office in 1932 and that no similar administration has been elected since.

Perhaps the high-water mark of the unawareness of those ruling our national economy in that decade was the opening paragraph of President Calvin Coolidge's message to Congress on the state of the Union delivered just eight months before the beginning of the great 1929-33 depression. Coolidge sent to the Seventieth Congress in December, 1928, these words:

No Congress of the United States ever assembled, on surveying the state of the Union, has met with a more pleasing prospect than that which appears at the present time. In the domestic field there is tranquillity and contentment, harmonious relations between management and wage earner, freedom from industrial strife, and the highest record of years of prosperity. In the foreign field there is peace, the good will which comes from mutual understanding, and the knowledge that the problems which a short time ago appeared so ominous are yielding to the touch of manifest friendship. The great wealth created by our enterprise and industry, and saved by our economy, has had the widest distribution among our own people, and has gone out in a steady stream to serve the charity and business of the world. The requirements of existence have passed beyond the standard of necessity into the region of luxury. Enlarging production is consumed by an increasing demand at home and an expanding commerce abroad. The country can regard the present with satisfaction and anticipate the future with optimism.

No unfairness is intended in presenting the facts of what leaders in the decade of 1920-30 did; for the state of unawareness and the recklessness and irresponsibility which stemmed from that period does not tell the full story of the proponents of the old order. I have said that in this period, as in former ones, there was a deep cleavage between the philosophy of the common people and that of those who lived on the returns from income-producing property. At times, the actions of both groups have been marked with folly, irresponsibility and corruption. The actual philosophy of the latter group is clear and comprehensive and it is only fair to outline it briefly, in contrast to the four important developments in the thinking and actions of the people themselves in the world of Franklin Roosevelt.

There are four predominant tenets of the conservative doctrine. One is the so-called "American System," which firmly believes in the inequality of men, and the inevitability of insecurity in life and of large numbers of poor people. Such quotations as "The poor ye always have with you," and "The Lord must have loved the poor people, because he made so many of them," serve to bolster this tenet.

The second is (and some consider this a contradiction of the first) that this is a land of opportunity for all, in which everyone by the exercise of his energy can achieve success; and that poverty is due to personal laziness and general worthlessness. This tenet includes the thought, so well expressed by Lord Macaulay, that the poor or common people are unreliable and need to be ruled by their betters.

The third is that any form of co-operative endeavor by the people to achieve mutual security destroys human incentive, which is built on fear; and also ruins character, which is based on self-dependence rather than on mutual reliance.

[103]

The fourth is that any form of co-operative endeavor in which the government is used as an instrument destroys individual liberties and fundamental freedoms, because it imposes regimentation on the people, and reposes authority in bureaucrats whose decisions are based on self-seeking motives, rather than retaining authority in bankers, magnates and others, whose motives are necessarily more unselfish.

Because these issues are current, it is outside the province of this work to try to defend or attack either group by attempting to define God's opinions on the subject. The verdict of the people, as history unfolds, will clarify these matters, for I am firmly convinced that "the voice of the people is the voice of God."

My purpose in stating the opposing viewpoint is to place Franklin Roosevelt's work in an understandable context of the world in which he lived and died. Throughout his Presidency, he stood for and tried to bring to fruition the first three of the developments that have been named on page 88, embodying their spirit finally in what he termed the Second Bill of Rights. In his last years, the fourth development, world co-operation and unity, came to the fore.

It is a striking realization that the four Presidents who are popularly considered the greatest in our history all shared during their respective Presidencies two deep convictions. The first was that they had a God-bestowed responsibility rising above all temporary issues, to preserve and defend the basic ideals of democracy on which our nation was founded. The other was the belief that during their terms of office overwhelming emergencies existed which threatened these ideals and made all-out action necessary.

The reader may recall the words of George Washington:

. . . the preservation of the sacred fire of liberty and the destiny of the republican model of government are justly considered, perhaps, as deeply, as finally, staked on the experiment intrusted to the hands of the American people.

At Gettysburg, Abraham Lincoln said:

Now we are engaged in a great civil war, testing whether that nation or any nation so conceived and so dedicated can long endure. . . . It is for us the living . . . that we here highly resolve . . . that government of the people, by the people, for the people shall not perish from the earth.

When Woodrow Wilson asked Congress for a declaration of war in 1916, he said:

To such a task we dedicate our lives, our fortunes, everything that we are and everything that we have, with the pride of those who know that the day has come when America is privileged to spend her blood and her might for the principles that gave her birth and happiness and peace which she has treasured. . . . The world must be made safe for democracy.

And Franklin Roosevelt in 1936 said:

There is a mysterious cycle in human events. To some generations much is given. Of other generations much is expected. This generation of Americans has a rendezvous with destiny. . . . We are fighting to save a great and precious form of government for ourselves and for the world.

When Franklin Roosevelt was first nominated in 1932, he used the phrases which gave a label to his whole administration and which expressed the motivating force of his efforts. They were:

I pledge you—I pledge myself—to a new deal for the American people. Let us all here assembled constitute ourselves prophets of a new order of competence and of courage. This is more than a political campaign: it is a call to arms. Give me your help not to win votes alone, but to win in this crusade to restore America to its own people.

Three months before, he had expressed the same theme in different words:

These unhappy times call for the building of plans that rest upon the forgotten, the unorganized but the indispensable units of economic power . . . that build from the bottom up and not from the top down, that put their faith once more in the forgotten man at the bottom of the economic pyramid.

As the years passed, much was attempted, much was frustrated or postponed, much was accomplished. Franklin Roosevelt's legacy to his country in its domestic policies lay not only in measures which spread relative abundance to the common people throughout the nation (without impairing the abundance of more prosperous groups), but also in the document which he called our Second Bill of Rights. This he first read to Congress in January, 1944. Because I do not think that any study of our people under God would be complete without it, I quote it here:

We have come to a clear realization of the fact that true individual freedom cannot exist without economic security and independence. Necessitous men are not free men. People who are hungry and out of a job are the stuff of which dictatorships are made.

In our day these economic truths have become accepted as

self evident. We have accepted so to speak a second Bill of Rights under which a new basis of security and prosperity can be established for all regardless of station, race or creed. Among these are:

The right to a useful and remunerative job in the industries or shops or mines of the nation.

The right to earn enough to provide adequate food and clothing and recreation.

The right of every farmer to raise and sell his products at a return which will give him and his family a decent living.

The right of every business man, large and small, to trade in an atmosphere of freedom from unfair competition and domination by monopolies at home and abroad.

The right of every family to a decent home.

The right to adequate medical care and the opportunity to achieve and enjoy good health.

The right to adequate protection from the economic fears of old age, sickness, accident and unemployment.

The right to a good education.

All of these rights spell security. And after this war is won we must be prepared to move forward in the implementation of these rights to new goals of human happiness and well being. America's own rightful place in the world depends in large part upon how fully these and similar rights have been carried into practice for our citizens. For unless there is security here at home there cannot be lasting peace in the world.

The war effort brought not only victory, but also the creation of the United Nations and the promulgation of the Atlantic Pact, making real the development of world cooperation. Like the other developments of today's world, these stem back to the past ages of mankind in many ways, but particularly to the first days of the United States. George Washington made many startling statements in his time, but none more startling than this, for perhaps no such statement had ever been made before in the Western hemisphere by a government head:

My first wish is to see this plague to mankind banished from the earth, and the sons and daughters of this world employed in more pleasing and innocent amusements than in preparing implements and exercising them for the destruction of mankind.

What has been developed in recent years is an outgrowth of that sentiment, strong in the United States throughout its history, and an expansion of the concept of the fundamental brotherhood of the people of the whole world.

And so we reach the end of our account of the three hundred million people who have made up the population of the United States, half of them living today. What is the ultimate destiny to this strange conglomeration of human beings, gathered from all the regions of the globe, who have, under God, forged new ways of life, new patterns of conduct, new realizations of the possibilities and the richness of existence in the world which God has created? I do not know, nor do you. I do know that all the citizens of today are more important than any segment of them. I know that the two or more billion human beings in the world, including our own population, are more important as a whole than any segment of them.

This, I believe, is the lesson that God has taught us. Our Constitution is the companion of all of us, and perhaps of all of the people of the world, in the furtherance of our political, social and economic needs. And God stands ready to give the people of the world the strength which they ask.

III. OUR LEADERS UNDER GOD

OUR PRESIDENTS AS HUMAN BEINGS

ACCOMPANYING THE QUOTATIONS from our Presidents are brief statements of some of the facts about their lives and comments on some of their personal attributes. No one has yet discovered a formula for becoming President or a set pattern that our Presidents have followed in their lives. Thirty-two of the 300,000,000 people who have lived in the United States have reached the Presidency, and each must be considered as an individual. So-called accident has sometimes played a part in their lives, perhaps chance, but each in himself has shown unusual personal power. In their expressions about God and our national destiny, they have probably expressed more fundamental agreement than in any other field.

The ages of the Presidents at their first inaugurations have ranged from forty-two to sixty-eight. Eight were between forty-two and fifty; eighteen were from fifty-one to sixty; and six between sixty-one and sixty-eight. Four were not elected to the office, merely serving out the terms of Presidents who died. Sixteen were elected once, eleven twice, and one four times. Had each President served one full term, by 1950 there would have been forty-one. As

[111]

it has happened, there have been thirty-two, serving from one month to a little more than twelve years.

Seven Presidents died in office, three of whom were assassinated. Of the others, six died within five years of leaving the Presidency, but thirteen lived between eleven and twenty-four years after their terms. Nine Presidents were defeated for re-election. Only one, Cleveland, served two terms which were not continuous.

One father and his son became Presidents, and one grandfather and grandson; the two Roosevelts were fourth cousins once removed. This is the closest approach we have had so far to family succession in the Presidency. One President, George Washington, was one of the wealthiest men in the nation, and several others have been wealthy; some of the others have been among the poorest in finances. One President, Buchanan, was a bachelor, and four Presidents were married twice. Eight Presidents had no children, and the rest between one and sixteen apiece.

Three Presidents did not claim any religious affiliations. By membership or frequent attendance, nine are considered to have been Episcopalians, five Presbyterians, four Methodists, four Unitarians, two Dutch Reformed, two Baptists, and one each a Friend (Quaker), Congregationalist and Disciple.

One President was born on July 4, and three died on July 4. Two Presidents were signers of the Declaration of Independence, and two others were signers of the Constitution. Ten Presidents had been Army generals, and others had seen military service.

That we may fulfil with the greatest exactitude all our engagements: foreign and domestic, to the utmost of our abilities whensoever, and in whatsoever manner they are pledged: for in public, as in private life, I am persuaded that honesty will be found to be the best policy.

That we may avoid connecting ourselves with the Politics of any Nation, farther than shall be found necessary to regulate our own trade; in order that commerce may be placed upon a stable footing — our merchants know their rights — and the government the ground on which those rights are to be supported. —

Courtesy of The New York State Library

Students credit much of Washington's Farewell Address to Hamilton and others, but the words here presented are Washington's own, written in his own handwriting before he handed his copy over to others to revise and augment. There are few men in world history whose character and actions fit so well the words "honesty is the best policy." It is only on such a cornerstone that democracy can survive.

Few men knew better from experience than Washington that the development of a nation is a never-ending series of struggles. The American forces under his command in the Revolution fought for eight years before victory was won. No sooner had peace been achieved than the new federation of states began to fall apart, and six years more passed before enough unity was achieved to organize a national government under the Constitution. Then came eight years more of struggle as the nation underwent the dangers of a new war and the menace of internal rebellion. Through all these crises, Washington was sustained by profound faith, infinite patience and a consciousness of the supreme importance of a free world, all of which are reflected in the words quoted here.

★

OUR FIRST PRESIDENT   George Washington was President from April 30, 1789, to March 4, 1797. He was born February 22, 1732, at Bridges Creek, Virginia, and died, at the age of sixty-seven, at Mount Vernon, Virginia, December 14, 1799. He was fifty-seven when first inaugurated. After his Presidency, he lived for two years and ten months. He married Martha D. Custis in 1759. He had no children. He was an Episcopalian. The approximate population in his administration rose from 3,900,000 to 4,800,000. When he was inaugurated there were thirteen states. Vermont, Kentucky and Tennessee were added to the Union while he was President.

GEORGE WASHINGTON

"No people can be bound to acknowledge and adore the Invisible Hand which conducts the affairs of men more than those of the United States. Every step by which they have advanced to the character of an independent nation seems to have been distinguished by some token of providential agency; and in the important revolution just accomplished in the system of their united government the tranquil deliberations and voluntary consent of so many distinct communities from which the event has resulted cannot be compared with the means by which most governments have been established without some return of pious gratitude, along with an humble anticipation of the future blessings which the past seems to presage . . .

". . . the preservation of the sacred fire of liberty and the destiny of the republican model of government are justly considered, perhaps, as deeply, as finally, staked on the experiment intrusted to the hands of the American people."

FIRST INAUGURAL ADDRESS
April 30, 1789

Just as Washington typified the early Southern land-holding aristocracy, John Adams typified the early Northern intellectual aristocracy. By the time he became President, Adams found the surge toward a popular democracy (threatening in the time of Washington, but far more active now) ready to engulf his more conservative views, and he lost his campaign for re-election in a bitter contest. He retired to private life, and in his later years acquired a close and affectionate friendship with his ancient foe, Thomas Jefferson. He lived to see his son, John Quincy Adams, elected President. John Adams and Thomas Jefferson died on the same day, the fiftieth anniversary of the signing of the Declaration of Independence, which both had shared in planning and creating.

★

OUR SECOND PRESIDENT   John Adams was President from March 4, 1797, to March 4, 1801. He was born October 30, 1735, at Braintree, Massachusetts, and died, at the age of ninety, at Quincy, Massachusetts, July 4, 1826. He was sixty-one when inaugurated. After his Presidency, he lived for twenty-four years. He married Abigail Smith in 1764. He had five children. He was a Congregationalist and became a Unitarian. The approximate population during his administration rose from 4,800,-000 to 5,500,000. When he was inaugurated there were sixteen states.

JOHN ADAMS

"In a humble reliance on Divine Providence we may rest assured that . . . the independence of our country cannot be diminished, its dignity degraded, or its glory tarnished by any nation or combination of nations, whether friends or enemies."

John Adams

MESSAGE TO THE SENATE
May 24, 1797

The making of the Louisiana Purchase by Thomas Jefferson and the issuance of the Emancipation Proclamation by Abraham Lincoln, are considered the two boldest and most daring individual acts of any of our Presidents. While later these moves were sustained and approved, each of the two men acted without specific Constitutional authority or Congressional permission. Both deeds were of supreme importance in the building of our nation. Jefferson was a scholar, a diplomat, an eloquent writer and perhaps the most profound philosopher of the roots of democracy who has ever lived. His rising to the occasion when dramatic, immediate action was needed—action for which he must take sole responsibility and for which he must risk the danger of personal disgrace and even conviction for impeachment—is an illustration of how strength is given to us to face a crisis bravely.

★

OUR THIRD PRESIDENT Thomas Jefferson was President from March 4, 1801, to March 4, 1809. He was born April 13, 1743, at Shadwell, Virginia, and died, at the age of eighty-three, at Monticello, Virginia, July 4, 1826. He was fifty-seven when first inaugurated. After his Presidency, he lived for seventeen years. He married Martha W. Skelton in 1772. He had six children. He claimed no religious affiliation. The approximate population during his administration rose from 5,500,000, to 7,000,000. When he was inaugurated, there were sixteen states. Ohio was added to the Union while he was President.

THOMAS JEFFERSON

"I shall need, too, the favor of the Being in whose hands we are, who led our fathers, as Israel of old, from their native land and planted them in a country flowing with all the necessaries and comforts of life; who has covered our infancy with His Providence and our riper years with His wisdom and power, and to whose goodness I ask you to join in supplication with me that He will so enlighten the minds of your servants, guide their councils, and prosper their measures that whatsoever they do shall result in your good, and shall secure to you the peace, friendship and approbation of all nations."

Th. Jefferson

SECOND INAUGURAL ADDRESS
March 4, 1805

Madison was only thirty-six when he did the work that later earned him the title, "Father of the Constitution." He was active throughout the years of the Revolution; tried to avert the impending anarchy arising after victory; was the chief architect of the document which is still the charter of our government; fought unceasingly for the ratification of the document; proposed the amendments now known as the Bill of Rights; and saw our national government begin and flourish under the administration of George Washington. Twenty-one years after he signed the Constitution, he was called on to become President himself, and a few years later he found our country once more at war with England, and all that he had helped to build in peril of destruction. We can only guess what melancholy thoughts and tragic feelings passed through his mind and heart. But he did not falter, and our nation emerged greater and stronger than ever.

★

OUR FOURTH PRESIDENT James Madison was President from March 4, 1809, to March 4, 1817. He was born March 16, 1751, at Port Conway, Virginia, and died, at the age of eighty-five, at Montpelier, Virginia, June 28, 1836. He was fifty-seven when first inaugurated. After his Presidency, he lived for nineteen years. He married Dolly P. Todd in 1794. He had no children. He was an Episcopalian. The approximate population in his administration rose from 7,000,000 to 8,900,000. When he was inaugurated, there were seventeen states. Louisiana and Indiana were added to the Union while he was President.

JAMES MADISON

*"The contest in which the United States are engaged
appeals for its support to every motive that can animate
an uncorrupted and enlightened people—to the love of
country; to the pride of liberty; . . . and, finally, to the
sacred obligation of transmitting entire to future generations that precious patrimony of national rights and independence which is held in trust by the present from the
goodness of Divine Providence."*

James Madison

MESSAGE TO CONGRESS
May 22, 1809

[121]

As can be guessed from his words quoted here, Monroe was President during a period known in our history as "the era of good feeling." It was not Monroe's role in our history to penetrate the turbulent struggle beneath the surface or even to perceive it. In life, each of us has a different job and different responsibilities. What Monroe did perceive and what he acted on with magnificent results was an entirely new international situation: the rise in Latin American countries of the same flaming desire for independence that had crystallized in the United States a half century before—and the apparent intention of European powers to intervene and to crush any such movements. The issuance of the simple statement now called the Monroe Doctrine, guaranteeing our neighboring peoples from attack and suppression, was one of the great turning points in our history, and the official beginning of our policy of acting in terms of world citizenship.

★

OUR FIFTH PRESIDENT   James Monroe was President from March 4, 1817, to March 4, 1825. He was born April 28, 1758, in Westmoreland County, Virginia, and died, at the age of seventy-three, at New York City, July 4, 1831. He was fifty-eight when first inaugurated. After his Presidency, he lived for fourteen years. He married Elizabeth Kortright in 1786. He had two children. He was an Episcopalian. The approximate population in his administration rose from 8,900,000 to 11,300,000. When he was inaugurated, there were nineteen states. Mississippi, Illinois, Alabama, Maine and Missouri were added to the Union while he was President.

JAMES MONROE

"When, then, we take into view the prosperous and happy condition of our country in all the great circumstances which constitute the felicity of a nation—every individual in the full enjoyment of his rights, the Union blessed with plenty and rapidly rising to greatness under a National Government . . . it is impossible to behold so gratifying, so glorious a spectacle without being penetrated with the most profound and grateful acknowledgements to the Supreme Author of all Good for such manifold and inestimable blessings."

James Monroe

MESSAGE TO CONGRESS
November 15, 1820

[123]

It was the curious fate of John Quincy Adams to follow in his father's footsteps in a surprising number of ways. Like his father, John Adams, he was minister to various European countries; became President at a time of popular and violent protest at conservative policies; was defeated for re-election by the leader of the movement for the common people, Andrew Jackson (his father had been defeated by the earlier leader, Thomas Jefferson); and lived for many years after his defeat. But unlike his father, he did not retire from public life, instead serving seventeen years as a Representative in Congress, and doing the most important and constructive work of his life. He was wise enough, as President and in his later years, to realize that for each of us there is an immediate job to do, and that doing this job in the best way we can is the most important task of any human being.

★

OUR SIXTH PRESIDENT John Quincy Adams was President from March 4, 1825, to March 4, 1829. He was born July 11, 1767, at Quincy, Massachusetts, and died, at the age of eighty, at Washington, D.C., February 23, 1848. He was fifty-seven when inaugurated. After his Presidency, he lived for nineteen years. He married Louise Johnson in 1797. He had four children. He was a Unitarian. The approximate population during his administration rose from 11,300,000 to 12,600,000. When he was inaugurated there were twenty-four states.

JOHN QUINCY ADAMS

". . . the first sentiment which impresses itself on the mind is of gratitude to the Omnipotent Disposer of All Good for the continuance of the signal blessings of his Providence, and especially for that health which to an unusual extent has prevailed within our borders, and for that abundance which in the vicissitudes of the seasons has been scattered with profusion over our land. Nor ought we less to ascribe to Him the glory that we are permitted to enjoy the bounties of His hand in peace and tranquillity—in peace with all the other nations of the earth, in tranquillity among ourselves."

J. Q. Adams

ANNUAL MESSAGE TO CONGRESS
December 6, 1825

Something new and tremendous happened to the American people, and in American history, when Andrew Jackson became President. Thomas Jefferson had been the first President who was out-and-out for the common people, as opposed to aristocrats. Jackson was himself one of the common people, and though his personal behavior and dignity could not be distinguished from those of an aristocrat, there was a real difference. He was not young—sixty-one when first inaugurated—and he was racked with pain from serious illness. His sense of duty was enormous, and compelled him to go on unflinchingly during his two terms in office. He had a profound conviction that his nation should advance in its awareness of the realities of human relationships. He did not believe that anyone in the past had said the last word on any subject, and he dared to believe that in his own day his fellow men were capable of creating new solutions to new problems.

★

OUR SEVENTH PRESIDENT Andrew Jackson was President from March 4, 1829, to March 4, 1837. He was born March 15, 1767, at Waxhaw, South Carolina, and died, at the age of seventy-eight, at the Hermitage, Tennessee, June 8, 1845. He was sixty-one when first inaugurated. After his Presidency, he lived for nine years. He married Rachel D. Robards in 1791. He had no children. He was a Presbyterian. The approximate population during his administration rose from 12,600,000 to 15,800,000. When he was inaugurated, there were twenty-four states. Arkansas and Michigan were added to the Union while he was President.

ANDREW JACKSON

"And a firm reliance on the goodness of that Power whose providence mercifully protected our national infancy, and has since upheld our liberties in various vicissitudes, encourages me to offer up my ardent supplications that He will continue to make our beloved country the object of His divine care and gracious benediction."

FIRST INAUGURAL ADDRESS
March 4, 1829

"You have the highest human traits committed to your care. Providence has showered on this favored land blessings without number, and has chosen you as the guardians of freedom, to preserve it for the benefits of the human race."

Andrew Jackson

FAREWELL ADDRESS
March 4, 1837

Van Buren was afflicted with a personal inability to sound as decisive in his words as he was in his actions. This is the reverse of the history of many of our prominent historical figures; and perhaps not a calamity, though in his case it brought many attacks on him and defeat when he ran for re-election. He was, oddly enough, exceedingly skillful in the use of words, and his difficulties did not stem from a small vocabulary or hesitancy in expressing himself. His really important public career covered three Presidential terms, though he himself was President during only the last of the three. During the administration of Andrew Jackson, he was perhaps the strongest moving force in bringing to reality many of Jackson's projects; and during his own term of office, other projects of Jackson were brought to fruition. He lived in difficult times, for forces greater than he or any one man were shaping our destiny.

★

OUR EIGHTH PRESIDENT   Martin Van Buren was President from March 4, 1837, to March 4, 1841. He was born December 5, 1782, at Kinderhook, New York, and died, at the age of seventy-nine, at the same place, July 24, 1862. He was fifty-four when inaugurated. After his Presidency, he lived for twenty-one years. He married Hannah Hoes in 1807. He had four children. He belonged to the Dutch Reformed church. The approximate growth in population during his administration was from 15,800,000 to 17,700,000. When he was inaugurated there were twenty-six states.

MARTIN VAN BUREN

". . . I only look to the gracious protection of the Divine Being whose strengthening support I humbly solicit, and whom I fervently pray to look down on us all. May it be among the dispensations of His Providence to bless our country with honors and with length of days. May her ways be ways of pleasantness and all her paths be peace!"

INAUGURAL ADDRESS
March 4, 1837

William Henry Harrison was the first of our Presidents to die in office. Two other distinctive features of his administration were that he was the oldest of our Presidents to be inaugurated, sixty-eight; and that his term was the shortest in our history, exactly one month. Despite his untimely death, Harrison's life was rich and full, both personally and in public service. One of his ten children became the father of another President, Benjamin Harrison, and he himself was the son of an earlier Benjamin Harrison who signed the Declaration of Independence. Three years old when the document was adopted, William Henry grew up to become one of the most celebrated of our military heroes, and later both a Representative and Senator in Congress.

*

OUR NINTH PRESIDENT William Henry Harrison was President from March 4 to April 4, 1841. He was born February 9, 1773, at Berkeley, Virginia, and died, at the age of sixty-eight, at Washington, D.C., during his term. He married Anna Symmes in 1795. He had ten children. He was an Episcopalian. The approximate population during his term was 17,700,000. When he was inaugurated, there were twenty-six states.

WILLIAM HENRY HARRISON

"We admit of no government by divine right, believing that so far as power is concerned the Beneficent Creator has made no distinction amongst men; that all are upon an equality, and that the only legitimate right to govern is an express grant of power from the governed."

W. H. Harrison

INAUGURAL ADDRESS
March 4, 1841

". . . and Tyler too," seemed during the Presidential campaign of 1840 to be probably the highest peak of fame Tyler would ever reach. Yet only a month after he had been inaugurated Vice President, he found himself the occupant of the White House, because of the sudden death of William Henry ("Tippecanoe") Harrison. Tyler was a man of strong and independent beliefs which did not coincide with those of the leaders of his (the Whig) party, nor with the trend of the nation against slavery. His term was a troubled one, because many of his actions failed also to please the Democrats. He withdrew from the campaign of 1840 after receiving a nomination from one segment of the Democratic party, and did not hold any public office for twenty years. Then, a few months before his death, he became active in the Confederate cause and was made a member of the Confederate Congress.

★

OUR TENTH PRESIDENT John Tyler was President from April 4, 1841, to March 4, 1845. He was born March 29, 1790, at Greenway, Virginia, and died, at the age of seventy-one, at Richmond, Virginia, January 18, 1862. He was fifty-one when inaugurated. After his Presidency, he lived for seventeen years. He married Letitia Christian in 1813; and Julia Gardiner in 1844. He had sixteen children. He was an Episcopalian. The approximate population during his administration rose from 17,700,000 to 20,200,000. When he was inaugurated, there were twenty-six states. Florida was added to the Union while he was President.

JOHN TYLER

"If any people ever had cause to render up thanks to the Supreme Being for parental care and attention extended to them in all the trials and difficulties to which they have been from time to time exposed, we certainly are that people. From the first settlement of our forefathers . . . the superintendence of an overruling Providence has been plainly visible."

John Tyler

ANNUAL MESSAGE TO CONGRESS
December 5, 1843

[133]

During the four years of James K. Polk's administration the United States acquired 1,200,000 square miles—about 40 per cent of its present area. A great part of Polk's time and energy was spent in consummating this goal, involving the voluntary annexation of Texas and support of its United States-born citizens in ousting Mexican government forces; a brief invasion of Mexico, ending in the Mexican cession of Far Western territories; and threats of war with England, culminating in an agreement bringing in the Oregon territory. It was a bellicose period, and the Mexican War was strongly opposed in the North. Polk himself was not bellicose, but joined heartily in the "Manifest Destiny" idea rising in the nation. One of our younger Presidents, he did not run for re-election, and died three months after his term expired.

★

OUR ELEVENTH PRESIDENT James Knox Polk was President from March 4, 1845, to March 4, 1849. He was born November 2, 1795, at Little Sugar Creek, North Carolina, and died, at the age of fifty-three, at Nashville, Tennessee, June 15, 1849. He was forty-nine when inaugurated. After his Presidency, he lived for three months. He married Sarah Childress in 1824. He had no children. He was a Methodist. The approximate population during his administration rose from 20,200,000 to 22,600,000. When he was inaugurated, there were twenty-seven states. Texas, Iowa and Wisconsin were added to the Union while he was President.

[134]

JAMES POLK

"I am happy that I can congratulate you on the continued prosperity of our country. Under the blessings of Divine Providence and the benign influence of our free institutions, it stands before the world a spectacle of national happiness."

James K. Polk

ANNUAL MESSAGE TO CONGRESS
December 2, 1845

Zachary Taylor was the second of our Presidents to be nominated and elected almost entirely on the basis of his being a celebrated war hero, with little regard for his political creed and platform. Though a Whig, which meant nominally that he was on the antislavery side, he was himself a large slaveholder in Louisiana. A son of his later became a Confederate general. Like the former President elected similarly, "Tippecanoe" Harrison, Taylor (who bore the popular sobriquet of "Rough and Ready") was not young when inaugurated. He was sixty-four, and William Henry Harrison had been sixty-eight. Like Harrison, Taylor died while in office. His fame had come later in life than had Harrison's, for only the year before his election he had been the hero of Buena Vista in the Mexican War. An interesting realization is that he was our President exactly one hundred years before the first publication of this sketch.

★

OUR TWELFTH PRESIDENT Zachary Taylor was President from March 4, 1849, to July 9, 1850. He was born November 24, 1784, in Orange County, Virginia, and died, at the age of sixty-five, at Washington, D.C. He was sixty-four when inaugurated, and died in office. He married Margaret Smith in 1810. He had six children. His family was Episcopalian, but he himself was not a church member. The approximate population during his administration rose from 22,600,000 to 23,200,000. When he was inaugurated, there were thirty states.

[136]

ZACHARY TAYLOR

"I congratulate you, my fellow-citizens, upon the high state of prosperity to which the goodness of Divine Providence has conducted our country. Let us invoke a continuance of the same protecting care which has led us from small beginnings to the eminence we this day occupy, and let us seem to deserve that continuance by prudence and moderation in our councils . . ."

INAUGURAL ADDRESS
March 5, 1849

"With the strict observance of . . . the Constitution, with a sedulous inculcation of that respect and love for the Union of the States which our fathers cherished and enjoined upon their children, and with the aid of that overruling Providence which has so long and so kindly guarded our liberties and institutions, we may reasonably expect to transmit them, with their innumerable blessings, to the remotest posterity."

Zachary Taylor

ANNUAL MESSAGE TO CONGRESS
December 4, 1849

Millard Fillmore was the President who saw our population reach the amazing figure of twenty-five million, and in the ten years before his Presidency he had seen such revolutionary inventions for human welfare as the sewing machine, vulcanization of rubber, the friction match, photography, and the epoch-making discovery of ether as an anesthetic. Yet three to five million American inhabitants were slaves, and that fact was more important to the American people than any other. Called suddenly to national leadership by the death of Zachary Taylor, Fillmore found himself in a national crisis which only war could resolve. He was unaware of the fact. Like most other leaders, he believed the whole thing could be settled by new compromises. Fillmore personally disapproved slavery and its extension, but the compromise he approved brought denunciations from the North, and from his own party, and victory to the Southern cause in the next election.

*

OUR THIRTEENTH PRESIDENT Millard Fillmore was President from July 9, 1850, to March 4, 1853. He was born January 7, 1800, in Cayuga County, New York, and died, at the age of seventy-four, at Buffalo, New York, March 8, 1874. He was fifty when inaugurated. After his Presidency, he lived for twenty-one years. He married Abigail Powers in 1826; and Caroline C. McIntosh in 1858. He had two children. He was a Unitarian. The approximate population during his administration rose from 23,200,000 to 25,700,000. When he was inaugurated, there were thirty states. California was added to the Union while he was President.

[138]

MILLARD FILLMORE

"... I cannot bring this communication to a close without invoking you to join me in humble and devout thanks to the Great Ruler of Nations for the multiplied blessings which He has graciously bestowed upon us. His hand, so often visible in our preservation, has stayed the pestilence, saved us from foreign wars and domestic disturbances, and scattered plenty throughout the land.

"Our liberties, religious and civil, have been maintained, the fountains of knowledge have all been kept open, and means of happiness widely spread and generally enjoyed greater than have fallen to the lot of any other nation. And while deeply penetrated with gratitude for the past, let us hope that His All-Wise Providence will so guide our councils as that they shall result in giving satisfaction to our constituents, securing the peace of the country, and adding new strength to the united Government under which we live."

Millard Fillmore

ANNUAL MESSAGE TO CONGRESS
December 2, 1850

In the decade before the Civil War, the job of being President of the United States was something like occupying an honored, thronelike chair perched atop a volcano on the eve of erupting. The three men who sought and accepted the job—not including Lincoln, whose inauguration coincided almost exactly with the opening of the war—were men with the tremendous personal faculty of ignoring volcanoes or considering that they could be controlled by a few simple measures. Franklin Pierce was the second of these three. Handsome, urbane, scholarly and genial, he applied himself to the immediate tasks before him. A defender of religious liberty, he won support among minority groups in the North. An opponent of anti-slavery agitation, he was also popular among Southern slaveholders and plantation owners. When not renominated for the Presidency, he made a pleasant and impressive tour of Europe.

★

OUR FOURTEENTH PRESIDENT Franklin Pierce was President from March 4, 1853, to March 4, 1857. He was born November 23, 1804, at Hillsboro, New Hampshire, and died, at the age of sixty-four, at Concord, New Hampshire, October 8, 1869. He was forty-eight when inaugurated. After his Presidency, he lived for twelve years. He married Jane Appleton in 1834. He had three children. He was an Episcopalian. The approximate population during his administration rose from 25,700,000 to 29,-000,000. When he was inaugurated, there were thirty-one states.

FRANKLIN PIERCE

". . . let not the foundation of hope rest upon man's wisdom. . . . It must be felt that there is no national security but in the nation's humble, acknowledged dependence upon God and His overruling providence."

INAUGURAL ADDRESS
March 4, 1853

"It is well that a consciousness of rapid advancement and increasing strength be habitually associated with an abiding sense of dependence upon Him who holds in His hands the destiny of men and nations."

Frank Pierce

MESSAGE TO CONGRESS
December 5, 1853

A lifelong bachelor is an interesting study at all times. Our only President to achieve this status was James Buchanan, and he maintained it throughout his seventy-seven years. In other ways, too, he seemed far removed from the ordinary currents of life which sweep men from one promontory to another. He was the last Democrat to be elected to the Presidency, except for Grover Cleveland more than two decades later, for a period of fifty-two years. Yet he seemed to have little consciousness that he was the last Presidential symbol of a dying cause, that of slavery; and that only when the Democratic party symbolized democracy again would it be powerful. Even though states seceded from the Union while he was President, he largely ignored the coming holocaust. But he was faithful always to the immediate duties of his work, and he maintained faith that justice throughout the world would some day triumph.

★

OUR FIFTEENTH PRESIDENT James Buchanan was President from March 4, 1857, to March 4, 1861. He was born April 23, 1791, in Franklin County, Pennsylvania, and died, at the age of seventy-seven, at Lancaster, Pennsylvania, June 1, 1868. He was sixty-five when inaugurated. After his Presidency, he lived eight years. He was unmarried. He was a Presbyterian. The approximate population during his administration rose from 29,000,000 to 32,400,000. When he was inaugurated, there were thirty-one states. Minnesota, Oregon and Kansas were added to the Union while he was President.

[142]

JAMES BUCHANAN

". . . I feel a humble confidence that the kind Providence which inspired our fathers with wisdom to frame the most perfect form of government and union ever devised by man will not suffer it to perish until it shall have been peacefully instrumental by its example in the extension of civil and religious liberty throughout the world."

James Buchanan

INAUGURAL ADDRESS
March 4, 1857

Abraham Lincoln was one of the very few Presidents who claimed no formal religious affiliation. His words quoted here, however, are evidence of the profundity of his recognition of God and his realization that departing from such recognition brings inevitable disaster. The words of his denunciation sound almost as if they had been quoted from the more memorable denunciations of the Scribes and the Pharisees made by Jesus. At the same time they breathe the identical spirit of universal love for mankind. The material and worldly rewards that came to Lincoln in his lifetime were meager. Even the grandeur and honor of the Presidency were accompanied by the agony of leading a nation whose brothers and sisters were in mortal conflict. And at the end he found only an assassin's bullet as his final earthly reward. Jesus too found a similar one.

★

OUR SIXTEENTH PRESIDENT   Abraham Lincoln was President from March 4, 1861, to April 15, 1865. He was born February 12, 1809, at Hodgenville, Kentucky, and died, at the age of fifty-six, at Washington, D.C., April 15, 1865. He was fifty-two when first inaugurated, and was assassinated in his second term. He married Mary Todd in 1842. He had four children. He claimed no religious affiliation but was a church-goer. The approximate population during his administration rose from 32,400,000 to 35,700,000. When he was inaugurated, there were thirty-four states. West Virginia and Nevada were added to the Union while he was President.

ABRAHAM LINCOLN

"And whereas it is the duty of nations as well as of men, to own their dependence upon the overruling power of God, to confess their sins and transgressions, in humble sorrow, yet with assured hope that genuine repentance will lead to mercy and pardon; and to recognize the sublime truth, announced in the Holy Scriptures and proven by all history, that those nations only are blessed whose God is the Lord.

"And, insomuch as we know that by His divine law nations, like individuals, are subjected to punishments and chastisements in this world, may we not justly fear that the awful calamity of civil war which now desolates the land may be but a punishment inflicted upon us for our presumptuous sins, to the needful end of our national reformation of a whole people? We have been the recipients of the choicest bounties of Heaven; we have grown in numbers, wealth, and power as no other nation has ever grown. But we have forgotten God. We have forgotten the gracious hand which preserved us in peace and multiplied and enriched and strengthened us, and we have vainly imagined, in the deceitfulness of our hearts, that all these blessings were produced by some superior wisdom and virtue of our own. Intoxicated with unbroken success, we have become too self-sufficient to feel the necessity of redeeming and preserving grace, too proud to pray to the God that made us."

PROCLAMATION
March 30, 1863

[145]

No President has undergone poverty and privation greater than that suffered by Andrew Johnson in his childhood and youth. His apprenticeship to a tailor when he was ten was literally like slavery, for he was chained to a table and a pair of shears. With no chance to attend school, he did not learn to read and write until he was nineteen, and then was taught by his wife. But he rose to eminence in political life. The Constitution and the Union were dear to him, as shown by his words quoted here. Though a Southerner, he sided with the Union in the Civil War, and was chosen as Lincoln's running mate in 1864. Yet his political tribulations came from the enmity of Northern political figures after Lincoln's death, and he was almost convicted of impeachment. But he continued in his career, and was elected to the United States Senate a few months before he died.

★

OUR SEVENTEENTH PRESIDENT Andrew Johnson was President from April 15, 1865, to March 4, 1869. He was born December 29, 1808, at Raleigh, North Carolina, and died, at the age of sixty-six, at Carter's Depot, Tennessee, July 31, 1875. He was fifty-six when inaugurated. After his Presidency, he lived for six years. He married Eliza McCandle in 1827. He had five children. He attended the Methodist church but was not a member. The approximate population during his administration rose from 35,700,000 to 39,100,000. When he was inaugurated, there were thirty-six states. Nebraska was added to the Union while he was President.

ANDREW JOHNSON

" 'To form a more perfect Union,' by an ordinance of the people of the United States, is the declared purpose of the Constitution. The hand of Divine Providence was never more plainly visible in the affairs of men than in the framing and the adopting of that instrument. It is beyond comparison the greatest event in American history, and, indeed, is it not of all events in modern times the most pregnant with consequences for every people of the earth?"

Andrew Johnson

MESSAGE TO CONGRESS
December 4, 1865

Ulysses S. Grant at forty-six was the youngest man ever to be elected President of the United States, except for Theodore Roosevelt. This is one of the many surprising facts in the unique career of the head of the Union forces in the Civil War. From the human point of view, the outstanding feature of Grant's life was his transformation from a hardware store clerk in 1860, when he was considered a failure, to one of the nation's most important figures three years later. Another memorable and inspiring feature of his life was his heroic and successful struggle, after he had suffered a financial disaster and while he was slowly dying and in constant physical agony, to write his memoirs so that he could repay his creditors and provide security for his family.

★

OUR EIGHTEENTH PRESIDENT Ulysses Simpson Grant was President from March 4, 1869, to March 4, 1877. He was born April 27, 1822, at Point Pleasant, Ohio, and died, at the age of sixty-three, at Mount McGregor, New York, July 23, 1885. He was forty-six when first inaugurated. After his Presidency, he lived for eight years. He married Julia Dent in 1848. He had four children. He was a Methodist. The approximate population during his administration rose from 39,100,000 to 47,100,000. When he was inaugurated, there were thirty-seven states. Colorado was added to the Union while he was President.

ULYSSES SIMPSON GRANT

"... I believe that our Great Maker is preparing the world, in His own good time, to become one nation, speaking one language, and when armies and navies will be no longer required."

SECOND INAUGURAL ADDRESS
March 4, 1873

"Amid the rich and free enjoyment of all our advantages, we should not forget the source from whence they are derived and the extent of our obligations to the Father of All Mercies ...

"By His continuing mercy civil and religious liberty has been maintained, peace has reigned within our borders, labor and enterprise have produced their merited awards; and to His watchful providence we are indebted for security from pestilence and other national calamity."

G. S. Grant

THANKSGIVING PROCLAMATION
October 27, 1875

During the term of Rutherford B. Hayes, the population of the United States passed the fifty-million mark, at that time a staggering figure for any Occidental nation. Also, the Southern States regained for the first time since the Civil War control of their own areas and people, when Hayes withdrew Federal troops completely from the South. Hayes was a Republican, as were all the elected Presidents from the election of Lincoln to the inauguration of Cleveland in 1885, but the Democrats had returned to power in Congress. Hayes was personally a man of force and character, and he devoted himself to reforms and improvements in the Executive Department. Though his election was by a minority of the popular vote, which led to a dispute as to his electoral majority, and though he was not nominated for re-election, he finished his term with credit to himself and his country.

★

OUR NINETEENTH PRESIDENT Rutherford Burchard Hayes was President from March 4, 1877, to March 4, 1881. He was born October 4, 1822, at Delaware, Ohio, and died, at the age of seventy, at Fremont, Ohio, January 17, 1893. He was fifty-four when inaugurated. After his Presidency, he lived for eleven years. He married Lucy Webb in 1832. He had eight children. He claimed no religious affiliation but attended the Presbyterian church and later the Methodist. The approximate population during his administration rose from 47,100,000 to 51,500,000. When he was inaugurated, there were thirty-eight states.

RUTHERFORD B. HAYES

"In all that concerns our strength and peace and greatness as a nation; in all that touches the permanence and security of our Government and the beneficent institutions on which it rests; in all that affects the character and dispositions of our people and tests our capacity to enjoy and uphold the equal and free condition of society, now permanent and universal throughout the land, the experience of the last year is conspicuously marked by the protecting providence of God and is full of promise and hope for the coming generations."

R B Hays

THANKSGIVING PROCLAMATION
October 29, 1877

[151]

James A. Garfield was the second of our three Presidents who have been assassinated. He was only forty-nine and was in the seventh month of his term when he died. As President, therefore, he did not have an opportunity to make any great contribution. But even though he was young, he had done much in his life which served as an inspiration in earlier days to hundreds of thousands, if not millions, of American youths facing hard struggles in life. A penniless worker on a canal boat as a boy, Garfield obtained a college education by his own efforts, was for a time a lay preacher, rose to be Major General in the Union Army, and was for seventeen years a Representative in Congress.

★

OUR TWENTIETH PRESIDENT   James Abram Garfield was President from March 4 to September 19, 1881. He was born November 19, 1831, at Orange, Ohio, and died, at the age of forty-nine, at Elberon, New Jersey. He was forty-nine when inaugurated, and was assassinated in the first year of his term. He married Lucretia Rudolph in 1858. He had five children. He was a member of the Disciples church. The approximate population while he was President was 51,500,000. When he was inaugurated, there were thirty-eight states.

JAMES ABRAM GARFIELD

"I look forward with joy and hope to the day when our brave people, one in heart, one in their aspirations for freedom and peace, shall see that the darkness through which we have travelled was a part of that stern but beneficent discipline by which the Great Disposer of events has been leading us on to a higher and nobler national life. But such a result can be reached only by comprehending the whole meaning of the revolution through which we have passed and are still passing. I say still passing; for I remember that after the battle of arms comes the battle of history. The cause that triumphs in the field does not always triumph in history. And those who carried the war for union and equal and universal freedom to a victorious issue can never safely relax their vigilance until the ideas for which they fought have become embodied in the enduring forms of individual and national life."

J A Garfield

ADDRESS IN THE HOUSE OF REPRESENTATIVES
August 4, 1876

The office of Vice President is greater than I ever dreamed of attaining," Chester A. Arthur told one of his advisers, according to a biographer. Without his knowledge, a greater office awaited him, that of President, for James A. Garfield was fatally shot in the first year of his administration. Arthur, a product of a strong political machine in New York, who had been appointed Collector of the Port of New York by President Grant and had later been removed by President Hayes, surprised many people by the way he met the unexpected situation. Perhaps his chief accomplishment was a program of reform of the civil service system. His wife had died a year before he entered the White House, and he seemed to be very lonely during his term. He did not run for President after the term ended, and died less than two years later.

★

OUR TWENTY-FIRST PRESIDENT Chester Alan Arthur was President from September 19, 1881, to March 4, 1885. He was born October 5, 1830, at Fairfield, Vermont, and died, at the age of fifty-six, at New York City, November 18, 1886. He was fifty when inaugurated. After his Presidency, he lived for one year and seven months. He married Ellen Herndon in 1859. He had three children. He was an Episcopalian. The approximate population during his administration rose from 51,500,000 to 56,-700,000. When he was inaugurated, there were thirty-eight states.

CHESTER A. ARTHUR

"An appalling calamity has befallen the American people since their chosen representatives last met in the halls where you are now assembled. We might else recall with unalloyed content the rare prosperity with which throughout the year the nation has been blessed. Its harvests have been plenteous; its varied industries have thriven; the health of its people has been preserved; it has maintained with foreign governments the undisturbed relations of amity and peace. For these manifestations of His favor we owe to Him who holds our destiny in His hands the tribute of our grateful devotion."

FIRST ANNUAL MESSAGE
December 6, 1881

Grover Cleveland is unique among our Presidents in having been the only individual to be elected for separated terms. Because of this, he has been often listed as both the twenty-second and the twenty-fourth President of the United States. Also, he was the only Democrat to be elected to office in the half century of Republican rule that began with Lincoln and ended with Taft. As a Democrat, he symbolized neither the traditions of the old South nor the rebellion against monopoly which was later to characterize his party. But as an individual, his straightforward honesty and directness of methods made him an outstanding figure among our Presidents. His two terms were marked by vigorous action in both domestic and international fields; and his vigor was illustrated by the fact that though he was defeated after his first term, he was elected again four years later.

★

OUR TWENTY-SECOND PRESIDENT Grover Cleveland was President twice; from March 4, 1885, to March 4, 1889; and from March 4, 1893, to March 4, 1897. He was born March 18, 1837, at Caldwell, New Jersey, and died, at the age of seventy-one at Princeton, New Jersey, June 24, 1908. He was forty-seven when first inaugurated. After his second Presidency, he lived for eleven years. He married Frances Folsom in 1886. He and his wife had five children. He was a Presbyterian. The approximate population during his first term rose from 56,700,000 to 61,800,-000, and during his second term, from 67,000,000 to 72,200,000. There were thirty-eight states when he was first inaugurated, forty-four when he was inaugurated the second time, and Utah was added to the Union during his second term.

GROVER CLEVELAND

"Our duties are practical and call for industrious application . . . and, above all, a firm determination, by united action, to secure to all the people of the land the full benefits of the best form of government ever vouchsafed to man. And let us not trust to human effort alone, but humbly acknowledging the power and goodness of Almighty God, who presides over the destiny of nations, and who has at all times been revealed in our country's history, let us invoke His aid and His blessing upon our labors."

INAUGURAL ADDRESS
March 4, 1885

"Above all, I know there is a Supreme Being who rules the affairs of men and whose goodness and mercy have always followed the American people, and I know He will not turn from us now if we humbly and reverently seek His powerful aid."

INAUGURAL ADDRESS
March 4, 1893

Ten presidents have been former Army generals. Benjamin Harrison was the tenth. His grandfather, William Henry Harrison, had been elected President in 1840 almost entirely because of his celebrity as a warrior. This, however, was not the dominant factor in the election of Benjamin Harrison. The tariff question, now happily out of politics in its original form, was then a burning issue. The attacks of Grover Cleveland on a high tariff were chiefly responsible for Harrison's replacing him as President. In turn, the extremely high McKinley tariff act during Harrison's administration enabled Cleveland to replace Harrison four years later. The period was one of rising strife between owners of industry and workers, and of clashes over the issue of bimetallism, and was an interlude preceding the historic clashes that were to come later.

★

OUR TWENTY-THIRD PRESIDENT Benjamin Harrison was President from March 4, 1889, to March 4, 1893. He was born August 20, 1833, at North Bend, Ohio, and died, at the age of sixty-seven, at Indianapolis, Indiana, March 13, 1901. He was fifty-five when inaugurated. After his Presidency, he lived for eight years. He married Caroline Scott in 1853; and Mary L. Dimmick in 1896. He had three children. He was a Presbyterian. The approximate population during his administration rose from 61,800,000 to 67,000,000. When he was inaugurated, there were thirty-eight states. North Dakota, South Dakota, Montana, Washington, Idaho and Wyoming were added to the Union while he was President.

BENJAMIN HARRISON

"No other people have a government more worthy of their respect and love or a land so magnificent in extent, so pleasant to look upon, and so full of generous suggestion to enterprise and labor. God has placed upon our head a diadem and has laid at our feet power and wealth beyond definition or calculation. But we must not forget that we take these gifts upon the condition that justice and mercy shall hold the reins of power and that the upward avenues of hope shall be free to all the people."

INAUGURAL ADDRESS
March 4, 1889

William McKinley was the third of our Presidents to die at the hands of an assassin. While the murder was unrelated to the political and national events of his administration, McKinley's whole Presidential service was performed in a period of turmoil, upheaval and violence, so that the quiet force of his personality and his steadfast devotion to his beliefs have to some extent been overshadowed by his colorful contemporaries and the dramatic events of his time. Yet the basic policies which he enunciated and followed have remained ever since the political creed of many millions of Americans. The chief event of his administration was the Spanish-American War, which was accompanied by a surge of imperialistic sentiment, but its aftermath in the half century since has been the liberation of large populations in the islands of the Pacific and the Atlantic.

*

OUR TWENTY-FOURTH PRESIDENT William McKinley was President from March 4, 1897, to September 14, 1901. He was born January 29, 1843, at Niles, Ohio, and died, at the age of fifty-eight, at Buffalo, New York. He was fifty-four when inaugurated, and was assassinated during his second term. He married Ida Saxton in 1871. He had two children. He was a Methodist. The approximate population during his administration rose from 72,200,000 to 77,600,000. When he was inaugurated, there were forty-five states.

WILLIAM McKINLEY

"Our faith teaches that there is no safer reliance than upon the God of our fathers, who has so singularly favored the American people in every national trial, and who will not forsake us so long as we obey His commandments and walk humbly in His footsteps."

INAUGURAL ADDRESS
March 4, 1897

The physical weaknesses which some of us have to struggle to overcome often seem to be blessings in disguise. Theodore Roosevelt was frail physically as a child. His determined, sustained and successful efforts to overcome this physical frailty made him one of the boldest, most colorful and intrepid of our Presidents. His vigor brought inspiration to the American people as has rarely been done before or since. Even in the consciousness of the children of today, almost half a century after he became President, the initials T. R. and the nickname of "Teddy" mean something vital. Theodore Roosevelt was the youngest President to be inaugurated in our history—only forty-two. He has remained always a symbol of those phases of Americanism which involve daring, courage and resistance to set patterns of conduct prescribed by tradition.

★

OUR TWENTY-FIFTH PRESIDENT Theodore Roosevelt was President from September 14, 1901, to March 4, 1909. He was born October 27, 1858, at New York City, and died, at the age of sixty-one, at Oyster Bay, New York, January 6, 1919. He was forty-two when inaugurated. After his Presidency, he lived for eleven years. He married Alice H. Lee in 1880; and Edith K. Carow in 1886. He had six children. He was a member of the Dutch Reformed church. The approximate population during his administration rose from 77,600,000 to 90,500,000. When he was inaugurated, there were forty-five states. Oklahoma was added to the Union while he was President.

THEODORE ROOSEVELT

"... *no people on earth have more cause to be thankful than ours, and this is said reverently, in no spirit of boastfulness in our own strength, but with gratitude to the Giver of Good who has blessed us with the conditions which have enabled us to achieve so large a measure of well-being and of happiness.*

"*Much has been given to us, and much will be rightfully expected from us. We have duties to others and duties to ourselves; and we can shirk neither. We have become a great nation, forced by the fact of its greatness into relations with the other nations of the earth, and we must behave as beseems a people with such responsibilities.*"

Theodore Roosevelt

INAUGURAL ADDRESS
March 4, 1905

[163]

From the time he was twenty-four until shortly before his death at seventy-two, William Howard Taft was continuously in public service, chiefly as a governmental official, partly as an educator. In this period of almost half a century, four years were spent as President of the United States. This small fraction of his forty-eight years of public service has since been considered in importance, as it was in proportionate duration, a relatively small part of his whole career. Yet in those four years he was one of the chief instruments by which a party split was caused, which resulted in the 1912 election of Woodrow Wilson. Thus for good or for bad, he affected the destiny of the United States and the whole world. His own espousal of the cause of international co-operation during World War I, and his later enormous contributions as Chief Justice of the Supreme Court, made him one of the outstanding figures of United States history.

★

OUR TWENTY-SIXTH PRESIDENT   William Howard Taft was President from March 4, 1909, to March 4, 1913. He was born September 15, 1857, at Cincinnati, Ohio, and died, at the age of seventy-two, at Washington, D.C., March 8, 1930. He was fifty-one when inaugurated. After his Presidency, he lived for seventeen years. He married Helen Herron in 1886. He had three children. He was a Unitarian. The approximate population during his administration rose from 90,500,000 to 97,200,000. When he was inaugurated, there were forty-six states. New Mexico and Arizona were added to the Union while he was President.

WILLIAM HOWARD TAFT

"The records of population and harvests which are the index of progress show vigorous national growth and the health and prosperous well-being of our communities throughout this land and in our possessions beyond the seas. These blessings have not descended upon us in restricted measure, but overflow and abound. They are the blessings and bounty of God."

THANKSGIVING PROCLAMATION
November 15, 1910

"A God-fearing nation, like ours, owes it to its inborn and sincere sense of moral duty to testify its devout gratitude to the All-Giver for the countless benefits it has enjoyed."

THANKSGIVING PROCLAMATION
November 7, 1912

Woodrow Wilson was the first Democrat to be elected since Grover Cleveland twenty years previously, and before that, since James Buchanan in 1856. The Democratic party had changed mightily over the years, though it still had many conservatives in its ranks and kept the support of the South. The spare, scholarly but vigorous figure of Wilson typified the rejuvenated party. He lashed out at monopolies, spoke of "The New Freedom" in which the common people would be the nation's first concern, proposed legislation to help labor in its struggles. In the crisis of World War I he developed his supreme contribution, the concept of world democracy and world peace. He saw his concept rejected and himself apparently discredited. Yet that concept is today an approaching reality, and the greatest hope of our age.

★

OUR TWENTY-SEVENTH PRESIDENT Woodrow Wilson was President from March 4, 1913, to March 4, 1921. He was born December 28, 1856, at Staunton, Virginia, and died, at the age of sixty-seven, at Washington, D.C., February 3, 1924. He was fifty-six when inaugurated. After his Presidency, he lived two years and eleven months. He married Ellen Axton in 1885; and Edith Bolling in 1915. He had three children. He was a Presbyterian. The approximate population during his administration rose from 97,200,000 to 108,500,000.

WOODROW WILSON

"I am sometimes very much interested when I see gen-
tlemen supposing that popularity is the way to success in
America. The way to success in this great country with its
fair judgments is to show that you are not afraid of any-
body except God and his final verdict. If I did not believe
that, I would not believe in democracy. If I did not believe
that, I would not believe that people can govern them-
selves. If I did not believe that the moral judgment would
be the last judgment, the final judgment, in the minds of
men as well as the tribunal of God, I could not believe in
popular government. But I do believe these things, and,
therefore, I earnestly believe in the democracy not only of
America but of every awakened people that wishes and
intends to govern and control its own affairs."

Woodrow Wilson

ADDRESS AT PHILADELPHIA
July 4, 1914

[167]

The sixth of our Presidents to die in office, Warren G. Harding, met with many troubles during the two years of his term—troubles with which he was unable to cope. As shown by his words quoted here, he was a man of deep religious faith. Unfortunately, he also had faith in some of his associates who proved unworthy of his confidence. To what extent the shock of discovering this helped to bring on his sudden, fatal illness will never be known. Trouble began almost as soon as he was inaugurated. Although he had been elected on the plea that the nation should "get back to normalcy," a serious depression developed, creating widespread unemployment and the loss of thousands of homes and farms. While efforts were being made to achieve recovery, the scandals of which some of Harding's close advisers were a part began to be made public.

★

OUR TWENTY-EIGHTH PRESIDENT   Warren Gamaliel Harding was President from March 4, 1921, to August 2, 1923. He was born November 2, 1865, at Corsica, Ohio, and died, at the age of fifty-eight, at San Francisco, California. He was fifty-five when inaugurated, and died during his term. He married Florence K. DeWolfe in 1891. He was a Baptist. The approximate population during his administration rose from 108,500,000 to 111,-900,000.

WARREN G. HARDING

"Liberty—liberty within the law—and civilization are inseparable, and though both were threatened we find them now secure; and there comes to Americans the profound assurance that our representative government is the highest expression and surest guaranty of both. . . . Surely there must have been God's intent in the making of this New World Republic. . . . Let us express renewed and strengthened devotion in grateful reverence for the immortal beginning, and utter our confidence in the supreme fulfillment."

INAUGURAL ADDRESS
March 4, 1921

One of the three Presidents who, after succeeding to office because of the death of his predecessor, has been able to win the next election on his own merits, Calvin Coolidge was famed for sincerity and intense determination. He was personally extremely shy and reserved. Moreover, he had been schooled in rigid political machine politics, and was generally believed to follow without question the opinions and instructions of the heads of his party. Yet, when faced by one of the greatest crises ever to confront a new President—evidence of gross, gigantic corruption among the heads of the party and their private backers—he acted boldly, swiftly and independently to bring an end to the corruption and to reinstate financial rectitude in the Government. He and his administration will always be remembered for the firmness with which he acted in a great emergency.

★

OUR TWENTY-NINTH PRESIDENT Calvin Coolidge was President from August 2, 1923, to March 4, 1929. He was born July 4, 1872, at Plymouth, Vermont, and died, at the age of sixty, at Northampton, Massachusetts, January 5, 1933. He was fifty-one when inaugurated. After his Presidency, he lived three years and ten months. He married Grace Goodhue in 1905. He had two children. He was a Congregationalist. The approximate population during his administration rose from 111,900,000 to 121,-800,000.

CALVIN COOLIDGE

"Peace will come when there is realization that only under a reign of law, based on righteousness and supported by the religious conviction of the brotherhood of man, can there be any hope of a complete and satisfying life. Parchment will fail, the sword will fail, it is only the spiritual nature of man that can be triumphant. . . . America seeks no earthly empire built on blood and force. No ambition, no temptation, lures her to thought of foreign dominions. . . . She cherishes no purpose save to merit the favor of Almighty God."

INAUGURAL ADDRESS
March 4, 1925

Our only living ex-President, Herbert Hoover, is one of the men of our time most admired by his fellow citizens. This admiration is not merely a sentimental tribute to past achievements, but an appreciation of the continuing public service which has characterized a great part of his life. He is one of our few Presidents who, with a humble beginning, achieved learning and wealth through his own efforts, and then dedicated himself to selfless public service, attaining international fame and affectionate regard without a thought of personal reward. It was his destiny, about which he has never complained, to reap the whirlwind sown by the folly of others and to be blamed for conditions created by others. Though his political opinions have not been shared by the majority of Americans for many years, he has remained steadfast to them, and has met this condition as he met former ones, by serving his country and the world with all his skill and energy.

★

OUR THIRTIETH PRESIDENT Herbert Clark Hoover was President from March 4, 1929, to March 4, 1933. He was born August 10, 1874 at West Branch, Iowa. He was fifty-four when inaugurated. He married Lou Henry in 1899. He has had two children. He is a Friend (Quaker). The approximate population during his administration rose from 121,800,000 to 125,600,000.

HERBERT HOOVER

"But I would emphasize again that social and economic solutions, as such, will not satisfy the aspirations of the people unless they conform with the traditions of our race, deeply grooved in their sentiments through a century and a half of struggle for ideals of life that are rooted in religion and fed from purely spiritual springs."

Herbert Hoover

ANNUAL MESSAGE TO CONGRESS
December 6, 1932

Already more has been written about Franklin Roosevelt than about any other President except Lincoln. How many volumes will appear in the next fifty or more years it is impossible to estimate. He still remains one of the most controversial figures of our times, but it can truly be said that his sudden death brought a deeper sense of shock and a more abiding sense of personal loss to more human beings throughout the world than has the death of anyone before in recorded history. Volumes of the future will probably give greater emphasis than before to the effect on his life of the torturing illness that crippled him, though he never publicly mentioned it, and his heroic and triumphant struggle against its inroads.

*

OUR THIRTY-FIRST PRESIDENT Franklin Delano Roosevelt was President from March 4, 1933, to April 12, 1945. He was born January 30, 1882, at Hyde Park, New York, and died, at the age of sixty-three, in Warm Springs, Georgia. He was fifty-one when first inaugurated, and died in office during his fourth term. He married Eleanor Roosevelt in 1905. He had five children. He was an Episcopalian. The approximate population during his administration rose from 125,600,000 to 139,500,000.

FRANKLIN D. ROOSEVELT

*"The Almighty God has blessed our land in many ways.
He has given our people stout hearts and strong arms with
which to strike mighty blows for freedom and truth. He
has given to our country a faith which has become the
hope of all people in an anguished world.*

*"We pray now to Him for the vision to see our way clearly
—to see the way that leads to a better life for ourselves
and for all our fellow men—to the achievement of His will
to peace on earth."*

Franklin D Roosevelt

FOURTH INAUGURAL ADDRESS
January 20, 1945

Harry S. Truman is our first President to be the leader of 150,000,000 Americans. His experiences bear many resemblances to those of former Presidents. Like Lincoln, he split rails and ploughed the soil as a boy. Like Jefferson, he is a skillful amateur musician (Jefferson played the violin). Like Theodore Roosevelt, he volunteered for the Army when long past the age of youth. Like six other Presidents, he succeeded to the Presidency through the death in office of his predecessor; and like only two others of those six, was himself elected later. But, with these and other resemblances, he is a distinctive personality and a unique figure. His direct, spontaneous approach to the people, his loyalty and determination, his courage in the face of apparently overwhelming odds, and his deep religious convictions, have made him one of the most popular of all our Presidents.

★

OUR THIRTY-SECOND PRESIDENT   Harry S. Truman has been President since April 12, 1945. He was born May 8, 1884, at Lamar, Missouri. He was sixty when first inaugurated. He married Bess Wallace in 1919. He has had one child. He is a Baptist. The approximate population during his administration has risen from 139,500,000 to an estimated 150,000,000 in 1950.

HARRY S. TRUMAN

"*We work for a better life for all, so that all men may put to good use the great gifts with which they have been endowed by their Creator. We seek to establish those material conditions of life in which, without exception, men may live in dignity, perform useful work, serve their communities, and worship God as they see fit.*

"*These may seem simple goals, but they are not little ones. They are worth a great deal more than all the empires and conquests of history. They are not to be achieved by military aggression or political fanaticism. They are to be achieved by humbler means—by hard work, by a spirit of self-restraint in our dealings with one another, and by a deep devotion to the principles of justice and equality. . . .*

"*As we approach the half-way mark in the 20th Century, we should ask for continued strength and guidance from that Almighty Power who has placed before us such great opportunities for the good of mankind in the years to come.*"

MESSAGE TO CONGRESS
January 4, 1950

IV. OUR UNIQUE HERITAGE

Treasy Dept. *nov 20th 1861*

Dear Sir,

> *No nation can be strong except in the strength of God, or safe except in His defense.*

> *The trust of our People in God should be declared on our National Coins.*

> *You will cause a device to be prepared without unnecessary delay, with a motto expressing, in the fewest and tersest words,*

Courtesy of The National Archives, Washington, D. C.

The above is a photostatic copy of a portion of a letter from Salmon P. Chase, Secretary of the Treasury, to James Pollock, Director of the Mint in Philadelphia, dated November 20, 1861. The motto, "In God We Trust," was first authorized by Congress for use on coins in 1864.

OUR UNIQUE HERITAGE

THE PRECEDING PARTS of this work have been an attempt to portray the United States in its development and in its religious attitudes as affecting that development. Through the Presidential quotations on God and our national destiny, and by a brief account of the American people and of their struggles, I have tried to show our nation beginning as a community apart from the rest of the world in its fundamental beliefs and political structure, and gradually integrating itself with the rest of mankind in awareness of the one-world concept.

My purpose now is to consider briefly the world-wide setting in which the United States was born and developed, and in which it exists at the present time, by expanding some of the preceding points that were only mentioned or left implicit. If there is any justification whatever for calling ours a "nation under God" in a special sense, it is because of our relationship to the rest of the world, both as beneficiaries of its past development and as contributors to its future progress.

We need to grasp, therefore, three groups of facts and ideas: (1) the former attitudes toward religious direction and authority for law; (2) the emergence of the United States from these older political structures as a novel and unique nation; and (3) the principles worked out largely in the United States as the first practical approach to world unity and co-operation.

Nations under Control of Laws of Religion and Similar Authority

When the Founding Fathers set up our Constitution they were writing fundamental law, which, as Marshall later said, "was to endure through the ages." Many of us see in the American Constitution a Heaven-inspired document. By any standard, the Constitution is the protector of the people's liberties. In other words, the doctrines in regard to the state and man's individual relations to the state are to be maintained by respecting the standards laid down in the Constitution. In honoring our Constitution and the Founding Fathers for establishing it, we assume that it has the sanction of Heaven, and that the Founding Fathers acted in accordance with eternal principles of truth.

Because of this, some might say that Americans are making a religion of our state theory or that we give to our Constitution such honor that we are thereby setting up a theocracy. In the case of some individual Americans, this may indeed be true. But real knowledge of the Constitution shows that such an attitude is not justified. As has been pointed out in preceding sections, the essence of the Constitution lies in its affirmation that it is the instrument of the people, who are sovereign, and that it can be amended at any time.

As we examine the structure of ancient nations, this basic difference becomes apparent. A rigidity, and a consequent sterility, obtain there that we have surpassed.

The concept of revelation from God as the force which sanctions law and government is confined in political thought to peoples who accept the Bible or the Koran: to the Hebrews, Christians, and Moslems. Nevertheless, the whole Western world, including ancient Greece and Rome, regarded law as having a religious sanction. In the development of law there was a time when all law was backed by what must be termed religion. In Western culture, the great lawgiver was God, and His will could not be questioned. In the East, since the concept of revelation was lacking, it was society that made of law a religion.

Justice, as we understand it, was not an independent, attainable ideal. Law included all morals. Even without the concept of revelation, the Orient gave to man-made law the force of revelation to such an extent that Confucius could describe his *Spring and Autumn Annals of Lu* as a book that would hold men bound for two thousand years. And it did. Hindu law became so binding ultimately by the caste system that it assumed all the force of Heaven. The law of karma which underlies all Buddhist theory, whether a product of nature or of Heaven, is eternal and inflexible. Both Hindu and Buddhist law hold the individual in the chains of fate.

In Greece and especially in Rome, the idea that law could exist outside morals and religion developed what we know as Roman law; but even so, Cicero could say,

I will boldly declare my opinion though the whole world be offended by it, I prefer this little book of the Twelve Tables alone to all the volumes of the philosophers. I find it to be not only of more weight, but also much more useful.

Thus in the mind of Cicero the Twelve Tables were more than human expedients. The Canon of Shun, the Code of Hammurabi, the Laws of Solon, and the Twelve Tables are really compilations of men's experiences in establishing rules for men in society. But if justice is attainable solely by faithfully adhering to such decisions of past generations, then we are all ruled by our dead. Rigidity can inhere in law whether it be a divine or a human imposition.

As Rome began to have contact with the rest of the world and other legal codes became known, a unity was recognized, and this unity formed the basis of what was called Natural Law. But a concept like Natural Law still leaves law's origin outside the state. Man is dependent on a power outside himself.

Another phase of outside authority for law and for leadership which appeared in various nations tells the same story. Superstitions, auguries, taboos and similar rites have no meaning to us, but to some people in some places these customs furnished ample basis for the belief that he who would direct the affairs of men must have the sanction of greater powers. One incident should suffice. When Tarquin, who left Tuscany to go to Rome to become the first Roman king, entered the city, an eagle, according to the legend, swooped down, snatched off his cap, flew through the air and then restored it to his head. That seemed sufficient sign and symbol to Tarquin and the populace as well. The story was enough to justify his reign. Whether the incident happened or not does not matter. It gave to Tarquin the sanction he needed in order to rule.

Birds and animals have been used throughout history

to add to the dignity of uniforms. Eagles had been used as emblems long before Tarquin's time, but as long as Rome lasted, the Roman eagle was recognized as a symbol of authority, an authority, too, which had the sanction of Heaven. Later on in Roman history Marius gave each of his legions a silver eagle. Thus the eagle was made to be representative of what the ancient writers called the "people's" legions. Julius Caesar adopted it, and with Augustus it became imperial.

The eagle which is now called the American eagle and is used on our flagpoles, on top of the mace, the symbol of authority in the House of Representatives, and in our symbolic art, along with the Roman bundle of sticks which Mussolini took for his symbol of fascism, tells history and can be traced back to some use in the past as an indication of a source of authority. Practically every American officer wears an eagle on his helmet or cap. The eagle on the American dollar, we must admit, is something more than art or a pretty decoration.

The Kaiser, the Czar and Napoleon used it. Its real origin in America may have been any of numerous sources; it was on the Austrian dollar which was current during the days of our Founding Fathers. The story of the American eagle is of interest to us here only to show how a symbol can be used without the connotation of supernatural authority.

In a very much broader way, and one which was wholly sincere, Herodotus gives us what most readers will identify as a Greek outlook based upon the concept of Divine authority for law. In this view, the destiny of the nation was closely tied to the fate of a person. The state was a personal affair. By the time of Xerxes, the Zoroastrian God, who was thought of as being as extensive and universal as light itself, was the God of Persia. The Persians often identified the symbol of light and Ahura Mazda as one. Herodotus takes it for granted that he does no violence to Persian thought and that his Greek readers will understand Xerxes if the justification of his conquests is put into words like these: "Persians! The law which I obey is no new law. It was learned from our elders. Persia, since Cyrus crushed the Medes, has not been inactive. God ever leads us on in our conquests to make Persia as wide as the heavens above." And giving a reason why he wants to conquer Greece, as Herodotus quotes it, he says: "The sun shall see no land upon our border. I will traverse all Europe and make all lands to be one land."

Throughout history and even in many places right down to today, God or the gods have been asserted to be the establishers of nations, a nation's protectors and, at many times, the partners of men in the accomplishment of national purposes. But just as there are differences among Ameterasu, the god ancestor of Jimmu Tenno; the God who led Cyrus; the god of the Persians; and the heaven that saved Greece; so, throughout all history, never before has there been a concept like that implied by Lincoln when he said, "This nation, under God."

Consider Kaiser Wilhelm's "God with us" and then note how he had his own picture put with that of God the Father, in the ceiling of the German hospice in Palestine. The Kaiser's slogan and his picture were cries for Pan-Germanism. Though the Kaiser was a Christian and imbued with modern thought, he and Xerxes were not far apart. Both linked the power of the ruler with that of God. Herodotus writes, "They [the Athenians] chose that Greece should remain free, and it was they who stirred up all the Greeks who had not Medized [that is, not joined the Persians] and they who *under Heaven* did in fact drive the King away." Thus Heaven supposedly helped to keep the Greeks from being subjugated by the Persians, and God helped Xerxes put Greece within the Persian borders so that the sun would shine on none but Persian land. We may turn even to the Bible and read, "Thus saith the Lord to his anointed, to Cyrus, whose right hand I have holden, to subdue nations before him." Politics and religion were inextricably mingled by these ancient people, and law was as of the essence of their deities.

In this connection, an experience of mine when I was a missionary in Japan affords still another illustration of God as the authority for human law. At one time, the Japanese Minister of Interior decided that for the sake of Japanese nationalism it was necessary to create a new Japanese religion. Many of us then in Tokyo, representing all religions, were invited to join in a conference. We were asked to help to work out a religion for Japan. It is not hard to imagine the replies of the various Christian representatives, which were similar to my own: "Our religion was not established by men, but by God. We, being merely men, cannot create another religion." The revelation-inspired religionists who had been invited were mostly Christians, although some Moslems were there, but there were, I believe, no Jews present because at that time there were no

Jewish communities in Japan. Incidentally, at this time Jewish communities in China also were almost nonexistent, in this case because they had nearly reached the last stages of complete assimilation.

The Japanese Minister of Interior who called the conference was not quite so innocent of religious differences as I have made it appear. But those who were creating modern Japanese nationalism on a Western basis assumed the necessity of putting a religious ingredient and religious loyalty into their nationalism because they were being aided by those of their own nation who were trained in the West, and by those Westerners who were trying to show the Japanese that they had in their own midst elements which could be used on a national scale, as they had been used on a feudal scale, to arouse willingness to sacrifice one's life for the Emperor. "For tonight you will sup with the gods," as Hearn put it, did as much to develop modern Japanese nationalism as Heine-Schumann's song, "Two Grenadiers," did in developing modern European nationalism. The Minister of Interior really did not want and did not need a new religion. What he wanted, and what soon came about, was a vitalization of Shinto to a stage at which it became a support for purposes of the state.

The devout old Russians, the Russians I knew so well in Japan, and later in Palestine, where I saw them as pilgrims, thought of the Russian state as existing primarily to support the Church. More than once I was told by a Russian religious zealot that Russia really had no national flag, save the flag of St. Veronica's handkerchief. There was no freedom of, or freedom for, religion in the old Russia. There was no proselyting. In the Russification of surrounding peoples and lands, adoption of the Russian language was not thought essential, but all were assumed to accept promptly the Russian state church. The "Little Father of All the Russias," as the Czar was called, was of prime importance. The Czar's ministers did not worry much about habits, customs or language, but they did like to see the spread of that influence and institution which sustained better than any others the concept of the "Little Father of All the Russias." Once such religious sanction was fixed, obedience in other respects could follow.

A thread that connects the concepts in various nations, from the most ancient to Hitler's Germany, is that of claimed attainment of perfection or of rigid fixity in political structures. Hitler's proclaimed "new order" was to last without change for a thousand years, just as Confucius predicted his work would bind the Chinese for two thousand years. Whether the authority for law was God, or the gods as personalities, or man-made codes of conduct, or an eagle sweeping down on Tarquin, the result was essentially the same. Perfection had been reached. In some cases, there had been a fall from this perfection, but the ideal status was fixed and nothing could be done to alter or impugn it.

China was an example of the latter idea. Many years ago, in the midst of my studies of the Chinese classics, I was struck with what I believed was the thinking behind Confucius' "Grand Course." The "Grand Course" was viewed as a historical recital of what we in the West might call the fall of man from a happier state to the present one of almost general misery. There was this great difference, however. What I have called the Chinese fall had nothing to do with religion. It was a political and economic fall. There were no Adam and Eve and there was no Garden of Eden. The "Grand Course" did not explain the origin of man. It assumed conditions when times were better. It is more closely related to the Western concepts of the golden and silver ages. The best times were past. The idea of man's growing into a better race had not dawned. The notion that man could make a better habitat was not envisaged.

One day I said to my teachers and my fellow students: "The 'Grand Course' is not history, it is a Utopia." To think of Confucius as a Utopia writer and not a historian shocked them as if they had closed an electric circuit. This led to arguments on my part about how Confucius never was a true historian, that he always wrote for a purpose, leaving out what he did not like and putting in only the things that proved his point or accomplished his ends. I became most unpopular among my little group. The commentators did not bear me out. Many student generations have come and gone since that time. So much have times changed that when I talked recently with some of the new Chinese, brought up under revolutionary thinking, I could hardly convince any of them that the Chinese had not always been in their thinking and outlook as they are today.

Such rigidity or inflexibility made it impossible for any nation to strive for universality, except in the sense of geographical conquest and expansion. Each national system of government was fixed, and there was no desire to extend its influence through reaching the minds and hearts of the people beyond the physical borders. It is true that with the advent of Christianity, missions came into existence, but conversion was largely restricted to religious attitudes apart from legal and political ones. The motive for conversion was the salvation of souls, primarily in preparation for life after death, and religion became an expression of an other-world philosophy rather than of a one-world endeavor.

The spread of Christianity over the world, from our standpoint today, is satisfying to us as a symbol of God's purposes for man in the enlargement of men's souls. Many of those devoted ones who carried the story and the meaning of the Christ to the four corners of the earth understood their missions, but in earlier days few made those missions function in such a way as to remake the land, to turn communities into places where a free soul could take on the enlarging of both self and surroundings in order that the dignity of man could attain its potentialities.

Putting a man on the Lord's side is an end that is satisfactory to religion. But the building of a new world where the souls of men already saved, in the sense of being on the right road, could grow and develop into men worthy of the Kingdom was not originally seen as also of supreme importance. Religions, in this scheme, have nothing to do with politics and economics on the mundane side of the fence.

Consequently, even on the human plane, in ancient times there was a recognition of two or more worlds instead of one. Great as were the influence of the Canon of Shun and the teachings of Confucius, the laws of China became so much laws for China alone that when extraterritoriality was asked by foreign nations who were breaking down

China's self-containment, the Chinese displayed no reluctance in allowing the foreigner to have jurisdiction over his own people. China never gave up its idea of the law of the place, but still, when the Chinese saw the foreigners in their midst, they could not refrain from the age-old habit of deeming all "barbarians" unworthy and of accepting, at least in their own minds, the theory that such people were not worthy of Chinese law. One penalty for the inflexibility of their law was that the field of its application was thus limited.

In the West, when capitulations were demanded on the part of the European countries in the Near East and in Africa, controlled as they were by Mohammedan thought, this same notion that a foreigner was unworthy of the protection of the local law had other aspects, but the recognition of a difference was there on both sides. Thus, universality was not even thought of. In ancient China, the Chinese Wall became as much a symbol of a foreign policy as it did a military protective instrument of defense. In the two periods when China was conquered, first by the Mongols and then by the Manchus, these conquerors tried to extend themselves, and they did, but in no sense on a universal scale. And as far as political thinking is concerned, each conquering dynasty was overcome by the strength of the philosophy of the conquered.

The suggestion may be made that universality was attained by Rome, during the times of the Roman Empire. This is not correct, because the Roman Empire was never universal. Roman law extended itself into many places, but even during the days of its furthest extension, in the estimation of those who were administering it or defending it, it was not universal.

Even in later centuries, when the community of nations idea was thought of and international law became recognized as having actual substance in the world and in the affairs of men and nations, it was never thought of as being universal. In fact, the whole Orient and Russia were outside its pale until the beginning of the twentieth century. When any system of law hardens into the given-once-for-all type of regimentation, it is bound to be exclusive.

The Influence of Earlier Nations on United States Development

Despite the enormous differences I have outlined in earlier states as compared to our own country, throughout all history there are threads of unity that are always discernible. The sixth century B.C. gave us the unities we find in the great religions of today, though we do not have the type of unity envisaged in our American use of the one-world idea. It is true that the ancient Stoics, despite their life in city-states, pictured all the universe as a single great polity. Then followed the espousal of the brotherhood of man taught by Stoicism and still later the Fatherhood of God, under Christian teaching. We can follow such thinking, as it grew out of Hellenistic thought, stated, for example, by Alexander, who remembered his Sophocles, and could say that he hoped to see the time when the people of the whole earth lived as one great family. But the governmental techniques for the fulfillment of this dream were generated only from American experience. It is one thing to hope for man's becoming a united family; it is another to make political conditions possible for such family life.

There was one attempt at universality which has had a tremendous influence upon the entire Western and Middle Eastern worlds. That stemmed from Alexander's conquests and the spreading of Greek thought throughout the then known world. Everything that has happened since Alexander's time has been touched with the influence he spread. Greek education mingled with monotheism, so closely identified with Hebrew thought, flowered in the scholarship of Alexandria and out of it all issued most of our Near Eastern and Western culture.

Alexander not only destroyed Persia, but he built an empire based upon universal ideas that captured all with whom they came in contact. In a sense, we today can say that his notion of universality laid the foundation for practically all of the attempts to reach that end that the world has tried since his time. Alexander accepted the profound insight of Sophocles, expressed in one of Antigone's speeches, that men unite well for war but never for peace, "Not to join in hating, but to join in loving." But that Alexander failed to act according to his own philosophy is proved by the fact that Persepolis was burned. Whether Alexander really did it is a question; in all his record, it is his only great destruction. Whether he or his followers did it just to avenge themselves on the Persians for their destruction of Athens does not make much difference today. The point is that Alexander, after all, was only able to unite for war and failed in bringing about a complete unity for peace. He glimpsed the truth, but not the way to reach it.

His vision, however, penetrated through the centuries and shed its glow upon the American continent.

Not only Greece, but, more directly, Rome influenced the Founding Fathers in their construction of a new type of nation. Since they wanted to found a republic, they turned to the nearest approach to a republic in the past. Fortune played a great part in the thinking of men throughout the whole of Roman history. But after the end of the Punic Wars and finally the crushing of Greece through the destruction of Corinth in 146 B.C., Rome became master of the Western world, and Polybius, a really great thinker and a penetrating historian, began dominating the thought of Rome. He recognized that it was not fortune that gave Rome her success. It was, first of all, a good constitution, a wise senate and a well-managed military. Rome was then at her best, when her politicians were incorruptible.

It was undoubtedly from this period of Roman history that Americans during the lives of the Founding Fathers took many of their ideals. They, of course, had long got over the idea that fortune ruled the destinies of men. They liked to think in terms of Heaven's helping us, but they did it as a Franklin would do it by accepting the Heaven-inspired aid in the sense that God helps him who helps himself. There is no doubt that the sterling citizenship of a man like Washington derived to a great extent from the finest specimens in Roman history. He represented the personification of what the Roman taught when he used the word "virtue." Roman manliness, Roman strength of character, Roman independence, were all there, and through honoring all of these virtues, the concept of a land "under God" could develop.

Greece and Rome were not alone in exerting influence on our forefathers. There were other sources from which our culture had developed, and these found a place under the Constitution or beside it. Therefore, Woodrow Wilson could say:

It would be a mistake, however, to ascribe to Roman legal conceptions an undivided sway over the development of law and institutions during the Middle Ages. The Teuton came under the influence, not of Rome only, but also of Christianity; and through the church there entered into Europe a potent leaven of Judaic thought. The laws of Moses as well as the laws of Rome contributed suggestion and impulse to the men and institutions which were to prepare the modern world; and if we could but have the eyes to see the subtle elements of thought which constitute the gross substance of our present habit, both as regards the sphere of private life, and as regards the action of the state, we should easily discover how very much besides religion we owe to the Jew.

To both Jewish and Christian habits of thought were added, among other things, our ready acceptance of the gradation of law and the process of appealing to higher law. Thus by the time of the Founding Fathers, while many Americans assumed the new nation had made a complete break with the past—as is reflected strikingly in the motto on the reverse of the seal of the United States, *"Annuit Coeptis"* ("He [God] has favored our undertakings")— *"Novus Ordo Seclorum"* ("A new order of the ages")—the past remained with us. We had taken for ourselves, in fact, all that Europe had to give.

To this rapid and incomplete summary must be added a word about another political structure that influenced the making of the United States. This was the structure of English colonies in North America, which grew into our nation. The reader will recall the impact of the New World on the colonists and the forging of a new way of life over a period of a century and a half. The nation that eventually took shape retained much which had developed first in England and had been further developed and modified by the colonists; and the Founding Fathers were also greatly influenced by movements in France during the eighteenth century which did not crystallize there until 1789, but which were increasingly important as the philosophy of "liberty, equality, fraternity" was worked out and promulgated.

The United States in Today's and Tomorrow's World

On an earlier page I have written that a serious "danger has threatened our country on numerous occasions. It is that even with the safeguard of separation of Church and State, belief in God and His apparent choice of certain peoples at certain times to act as leaders in human progress can intoxicate these peoples into disastrous confusion about their destiny. They come to believe that they are more than temporary leaders in human betterment; that instead, they have been divinely empowered to rule other peoples because they are members of a master nation or race. . . . it is a folly that has endangered the United States . . . sometimes bringing us to the brink of calamity."

This danger is always present. Indubitably it has wrought havoc in the past, and societies I have briefly sketched have

[197]

succumbed to it. In our own day the so-called holy crusades waged by Hitler's Germany, Mussolini's Italy, and the Oriental war lords' Japan have met with disastrous results. Despite their outcome, as I have written before, we hear from time to time in our own country murmurs that once again a holy crusade of some kind is in order, perhaps to be initiated by us.

It is vitally important in view of the peril that lurks within such arrogance that all of us consider our present and future relationship with the rest of mankind. Loose talk of world leadership makes a heady brew. Our admitted leadership in many fields must not be assumed to imply the ownership of other peoples and the mastery of their destinies. The principles of human relationships and basic governmental structure, worked out largely in the United States, are, in my opinion, the first practical approach to world unity and co-operation. To weaken or depart from those principles will be to waste the precious heritage which is ours. Our position of economic supremacy does not entitle us to make a God of ourselves.

While the American Revolution is a beginning to me, and has all the elements of a beginning that can permeate the world, it must produce a more perfect union at home and maintain its standards wherever its influence goes. Thus other peoples without shall not debase the fundamental American Revolutionary concepts, and create what might be called an "Americanistic" culture throughout the world. We must not choose, as a result of the two world wars and the responsibility that is now ours, to relinquish our hold on our sense of progress, to alter the meaning of liberty and to blend the corruptions that would ensue into a justification for our dominion. We are entitled to guide the world only on the basis of the same principles that have exalted us into a position of leadership.

My view is that our country is a link between the past and the future, between a past of slavery and isolation, and a future of freedom and world brotherhood. To use another figure, we constitute a bridge across which hundreds of millions of people may pass to new realizations of living, and these discoveries can help to unite the whole world, as its multitudes (including our own) pass across from old concepts to those that are new.

It is because of this feeling that I have outlined the political structures of past nations, both in their differences from our own and in their influence on our forefathers. It would be repetitious to outline the unique civilization which the American people have built, for this book has been devoted to that end. Our history declares it better than could I. It may be appropriate, however, to summarize here the unique changes in attitudes, in ways of living and in political structure that bear directly on our relationship to the rest of the world, with emphasis on their relevance to world unity and co-operation.

The first and most obvious changes have been in the status of human beings. Western religion has always held that the souls of all men are equally significant in the eyes of God, and are cherished with equal love. American history has extended this equality to the minds and bodies of human beings, proclaiming that all men are created equal and are equally entitled to justice, opportunity, rights and privileges, on the political as well as the spiritual level.

Another concept that has guided our history is the recognition of certain inalienable rights pertaining to each individual, which are superior to, and unassailable by, the laws of the state. These we call religious. The spiritual entity in man is guaranteed the possibility of spiritual expression. Any individual has the freedom to accept or reject any or all religion, or to change from one institutional form of religion to another without penalties imposed by society, as a whole or in part.

This is our doctrine of the separation of Church and State. Theologians may trace the source of this separation to the words of Jesus, "Render unto Caesar the things that are Caesar's and unto God the things that are God's." While not disagreeing with this interpretation of the text, I think it important to penetrate the surface of these words, in particular, of the reference to "the things that are Caesar's," in order to understand fully the Church-State relationship developed in the United States. "The things that are Caesar's," without such analysis, may be taken as implying that the rulership of men by other men is justifiable in certain areas of religious behavior. But this dictum is opposed to the American concept, which flatly denies the right of anyone to rule over anyone else in matters of conscience. This saying of Jesus, therefore, means that there is a clear distinction between actions subject to the will of the people and actions subject to the authority of God. When Jesus made his statement, he spoke to hearers who could not comprehend the concept of separation of legal systems. The law of the Sanhedrin could not permit that. The Romans, too, from another point of view, could not permit their laws to be divided into groups, with different authority for each group.

In practice, this has been accomplished by denying legal authority for any religious institution or its representatives to direct the affairs of human beings. In all those actions which affect himself alone, an individual may subject himself, if he so desires, to the tenets of any religion. Only in those actions which affect other people is he amenable to the state, whose laws he himself helps to make and carry out. Every man in being free in the presence of God achieves a corresponding freedom in his association with his fellow men.

In pursuance of this principle, the Founding Fathers separated Church and State in the national government, and over a period of many years, the individual states followed suit, making a complete break between political law and religious authority. The state had to do with the former. With the latter, persons within the state were free to follow their own conscience. Many have asked: "How can the thesis of a 'nation under God' be consistent with the fact that the American people are free in their political actions? Can we create a 'land of destiny' in the light of our notion of a free people in a free state?" The answer will be found in America's history. We have done it. The principle is no mere theory: it has worked and is working.

All religions have prospered in America. All religions have remained free excepting when, to state the restraint imposed by the Supreme Court, religion is used to justify what society has determined to be an immoral practice. Thus, even churches have made greater headway under freedom than when they have been an organ of the state. Though the influence of religion is thus made indirect, it is real and effectual.

We, too, see the worth of the churches in our daily lives and our communities; their value is not to be minimized or depreciated. The influence of the churches, in our big cities especially, is a stabilizing and a moralizing force. Without their unifying influence, our centers of population would be rent with racial, social and economic discord instead of being places of comparative peace. It is because of American freedoms of expression, speech, religious belief, economic rights to have and to hold and the right to come and to go, that American cities are accomplishing what thinkers and writers of other parts of the world thought impossible. To the great Catholic churches, both Roman and Orthodox, to the Jewish leadership, both Orthodox and Reformed, great and lasting credit must go for the making of American cities.

The mere fact that a man from Estonia and a man from Hungary can find common meeting ground in a cathedral or a synagogue accomplishes much. The line-up of "Fighting Irish" teams of Notre Dame or Fordham, in which Irish names do not appear often enough to be monotonous, illustrates my point. The Protestant churches are active, too, for they likewise teach American unity. I have given "Americans All" talks to many groups, where I was the only fair-haired, blue-eyed American present. But on talking to these "foreigners," I found that their words and acts reflected hearts and hopes as American as my own father's and mother's, who came from afar to find in America the answer to a lifelong prayer. I know of not a single church which does not daily contribute to the nourishment of American ideals for our body politic, but to my knowledge the state has never used the churches to accomplish political purposes. Such freedom seemed dangerous to dogmatists, but it has brought results. The state, of course, has laid down educational requirements for private schools, because it is within the province of the state to assure educational standards. But it uses no school to propagandize and to indoctrinate. Americans are quick to detect the difference between education and propaganda, and they know one from the other.

This separation of Church and State does not mean that God has nothing to do with the world. It does not mean that ethical principles belong in one compartment of man's mind, his methods of doing business in another. What it does mean is that for the religious and the practical life to fuse, they must be held apart. Religion meets politics and economics in the only place they may truly meet: in the heart and soul of the individual man. The condition which makes people capable of governing themselves is that no barrier be erected between the individual self and his free access to God. Only men who are spiritually free in one sense can be politically free in another. Popular sovereignty and religious liberty are, therefore, not two discoveries, but dual aspects of one and the same.

Democracy is a community of real men, and in a real man there is no distinction between conviction and conduct. Authentic spokesmen of the American way, therefore, have inevitably shed religious insights upon political situations. "With malice toward none and with charity for all" is manifestly an ethical ideal. But Lincoln intended it as no recipe for getting along with angels, but for practical guidance in dealing with rebels. Religion and politics can meet in the soul of a statesman, and that we are a "nation under God" has been due to the fact that our destiny has ever been guided by men who have discerned an obligation just at the point where freedoms met.

As radical a revolution as any in history was our transfer of authority in respect to law from codes decreed by divinely designated individuals or institutions to the people. Its importance lay not only in the novelty that it made the people their own rulers for the first time on record, but also that it inaugurated a dynamic type of government to replace all the stereotypes of the past. Rule by the people permitted a new factor to enter into legislation—change and progress. Before the United States became a nation, such an idea had never been thought of. Not until Condorcet gave the world the concept of progress could anyone make a governmental concept out of change. There were golden ages and silver ages, there were cycles, there were "falls" in the past, and Utopias in the future. But until the idea of progress dawned on men, there could be no "heaven on earth" except by fiat. The race might start all over, as it did in Noah's day, but progress as we understand it today was ruled out by the very lack of the idea whereby to conceive it.

But the idea of progress combined with the concept of

individual liberty shattered the figments of the past and sent static civilizations crashing. That actually occurred when the meaning of the American Revolution began to seize the minds of men. The American Revolution has not yet encircled the globe. But our Constitution is now the oldest document of its kind on earth and no change can be looked for anywhere which has not come to pass in response to American political experience.

The perfectibility of man and nations has seemed possible in many places and at many times throughout history, but the idea of progress logically renders perfection impossible, if we regard the culmination of events as a static state. "A more perfect union" did not end with the setting up of the Constitution. "Liberty" and "progress" are never fixed and final. Man will always be on his way, but never arriving. Always there will be tensions to be resolved. Revolution is the permanent state of humanity. Man must be continually striving. Conflict is the price of liberty. We will turn to a political end now, to an economic end tomorrow, to a social end on the next day. But the same righteousness will determine all our ends, howsoever we conceive them.

Only by recognizing the sovereignty of the people in the making of law and in its functioning within a nation can a condition of change and progress become a possibility. Any divine mandate lacks the elasticity required. We can scarcely imagine at the end of the Decalogue a final clause being attached to the effect that any or all these commandments could be abolished or amended at any time by a majority vote of their adherents. Such a clause is inconsistent with the acceptance of the Commandments as an eternal guide for our human conduct. Such ideals, therefore, constitute ends which are religious, but the means for their implementation, being political, must vary with conditions. Thus it is of the essence of our Constitution that they who have made it can alter it at any time. As we grow in understanding and in the technique of self-government, we can adapt our procedures accordingly. But such alteration does not signify that we have renounced our status as a "nation under God."

From the point of view of world unity and international co-operation, our history has revealed still another principle that is basic. Our governmental structure is adapted in a notable respect to extension throughout the world. The pattern whereby the thirteen states were brought together into an unbreakable unity can be used for the union of nations as well. The Founding Fathers worked out our federal system on the basis of allowing matters of purely local concern to be settled locally, but matters of common interest to be handled by representatives delegated to speak for all. That governmental strategy is still the source of our political liberty. It is the key to peace within a nation compounded of forty-eight states, and the same key might unlock the door of globe-wide peace. Thus, we have wrought as a result of American experience, a conception of government on which world organization can rest and embody the will for world unity when that will demands expression.

While men have dreamed of peace since the beginning of time, they did not engender a form of government which possessed the capacity to become world-wide, and, therefore, to insure the peace hoped for. No longer, however, is

the concept of world government a mere theory; no longer
is it based upon yearning and aspiration. The way to peace
is established in the world, whether or not the nations will
tread that path, through the remarkable American political
technique known as federalism, and through our discovery of dual citizenship. We have revealed for the first
time in history a governmental pattern that can meet any
situation imperiled by war. When the peoples of the world
are ready to submerge conflicting interests and narrow
loyalties in a larger view and an overarching harmony, all
the nations need do is to look to America as an example of
how the longed-for goal may be achieved.

Our own century has been marked by a development that
has been as new as it has been vast. Our domestic horizon
has expanded in richness and rewards. We have been led
to fresh intimate association with races of other climes and
continents. We have accepted mutually our responsibility
to one another. All mankind must prosper or perish together. Our co-operation with our fellow nations is by no
means restricted to acts of charity. We do not seek our
national interests solely. There is genuine recognition that
all peoples are our brothers, that we are theirs, that we are
involved in a common career. This destiny summons us, and
our answer will be heard for all time. When one muses over
the unique station which is ours as a nation, words of Woodrow Wilson uttered in June, 1916, to the students at West
Point seem inspired. They express everything I have been
laboring to say.

. . . America came into existence for a particular reason.
When you look about upon those beautiful hills, and up this

stately stream, and then let your imagination run over the whole body of this great country from which you youngsters are drawn, far and wide, you remember that while it had aboriginal inhabitants, while there were people living here, there was no civilization which we displaced. It was as if in the Providence of God a continent had been kept unused and waiting for a peaceful people who loved liberty and the rights of men more than they loved anything else, to come and set up an unselfish commonwealth. It is a very extraordinary thing. You are so familiar with American . . . history that it does not seem strange to you, but it is a very strange history. There is none like it in the whole annals of mankind—of men gathering out of every civilized nation in the world on an unused continent and building up a polity exactly to suit themselves, not under the domination of any ruling dynasty or of the ambitions of any royal family, doing what they pleased with their own life on a free space of land which God had made rich with every resource which was necessary for the civilization they meant to build up. There is nothing like it.

INDEX

Adams, John, 47, 68, 116-117, 124
Adams, John Quincy, 116, 124-125
Adams, Samuel, 45
Ahura Mazda, 186
Alexander, 193-195
Allen, Ethan, 46
Ameterasu, 186
Appleton, Jane, 140
Aristotle, 38
Arthur, Chester A., 154-155
Axton, Ellen, 166

Beecher, Henry Ward, 73
Beveridge, Albert J., 17
Bixby, Mrs. Lydia, 85
Bolling, Edith, 166
Bradford, William, 43
Bradstreet, Anne, 43
Bryan, William Jennings, 43, 91, 92, 100
Buchanan, James, 112, 142-143, 166
Burr, Aaron, 43

Caesar, Augustus, 185, 200
Caesar, Julius, 185
Carow, Edith K., 162
Chase, Salmon P., 180
Childress, Sarah, 134
Cicero, 184
Cleveland, Grover, 112, 150, 156-157, 158, 166
Columbus, Christopher, 4, 26, 27, 53
Condorcet, Marquis de, 204
Confucius, 183, 189, 190, 191
Coolidge, Calvin, 102, 170-171
Custis, Martha D., 114
Cyrus, 186, 187

Dent, Julia, 148
DeWolfe, Florence K., 168
Dimmick, Mary L., 158

Emerson, Ralph Waldo, 46

Fillmore, Millard, 138-139
Fiske, John, 57
Fitzgerald, F. Scott, 94
Folsom, Frances, 156
Franklin, Benjamin, 24, 40, 47, 51, 54, 195

Gardiner, Julia, 132
Garfield, James A., 152-153, 154
George III, 52, 77, 100
Goodhue, Grace, 170
Grant, Ulysses S., 148-149, 154

Haas, Bishop Francis Joseph, 4
Hammurabi, 184
Harding, Warren G., 168-169
Harrison, Benjamin, 130, 158-159
Harrison, William Henry, 130-131, 132, 136, 158
Harvard, John, 43
Hayes, Rutherford B., 150-151, 154
Hearn, Lafcadio, 188
Hemingway, Ernest, 94
Henry, Lou, 172
Henry, Patrick, 45
Herndon, Ellen, 154
Herodotus, 185, 186
Herron, Helen, 164
Hitler, Adolf, 53, 189, 198
Hoes, Hannah, 128
Hoover, Herbert, 43, 172-173
Hughes, Charles Evans, 24
Hugo, Victor, 99

[209]

Index